The Quality of Education
in Developing Countries

The Quality of Education

in Developing Countries

C. E. BEEBY

HARVARD UNIVERSITY PRESS

Cambridge, Massachusetts

1 9 6 6

This book was made possible in part by funds granted by the Carnegie Corporation of New York. The statements made and views expressed are solely the responsibility of the author.

Distributed in Great Britain by Oxford University Press, London

TO BEATRICE

FOREWORD

I first met C. E. Beeby in Ghana, where he was representing New Zealand at the installation of the President. He told me then that he preferred educational research to diplomacy—he was his country's Ambassador to France—and hoped to return to this field when he retired. I assumed that this was an expression of nostalgia unlikely to be realized, but this book shows that I was wrong. Mr. Beeby concentrates an extraordinary volume of diverse experience on problems which most writers side-step: most of us pay lip service to the need for quality in planning but, having advocated it, pass rapidly on to more tangible issues.

Mr. Beeby is in a unique position to illuminate all facets of educational development. He spent twenty years as Director of Education in New Zealand, in which capacity he was in charge of education in metropolitan New Zealand with its highly developed system of public education and also had responsibilities in the Pacific island dependencies, which were several generations behind. This laid the basis for an understanding of issues of development and planning which matured during his two-year spell as Assistant Director-General of UNESCO, in charge of UNESCO education programs. Mr. Beeby has served also as chairman of the UNESCO Board and in a number of other international assignments. To these high offices he has brought experience and his early intellectual interests—his doctorate is in psychology and he was for several years Director of the New Zealand Council for Educational Research. All this has given an unusual and vital flavor to his thinking, a tough yet sensitive empiricism which has defied the manifold pressures upon the administrator to achieve stereotyped solutions to problems. This extremely important book will, in fact, probably create additional difficulties for administrators, for no one who reads it can be satisfied with an easy answer to a universal dilemma.

A great deal of thought is now being directed toward educational planning, but for the most part we have been concerned with procedures for effectively expanding the quantity of education and we have ignored the implications for quality—a concept we have not even begun to define satisfactorily. This book adds a whole new dimension to what was beginning to become a sterile juggling with figures.

I can only add that Harvard University is extremely fortunate to have induced Mr. Beeby to spend a few years here while distilling the rich experience of a lifetime spent on the pioneering frontiers of educational development.

Adam Curle, Director,
Center for Studies in Education and
Development, Graduate School of
Education, Harvard University

October 27, 1965

ACKNOWLEDGMENTS

For so short a book, the list of acknowledgments is long, but its length is a true measure of my indebtedness. I am grateful to the Carnegie Corporation of New York whose generosity made it possible for me to come to the United States to start the book, and to the Harvard Graduate School of Education and its Dean, Theodore R. Sizer, whose equally generous policy enabled me to stay on to finish it. The Editor of the *Comparative Education Review* was good enough to allow me to use, without benefit of quotation marks, portions of an article of mine in that journal.

In a field where much has been done in practice throughout the world but little has been written, I have had to lean heavily on the criticism and advice of friends and colleagues whose knowledge of schools in other lands has been either wider or more intensive than my own. They include: Sir Christopher Cox, Freda Gwilliam, and Harold Houghton of the United Kingdom Ministry of Overseas Development; V. L. Griffiths of Oxford University; Rose E. Sabaroff and Robert H. Anderson of the Harvard Graduate School of Education; my colleagues in the Center for Studies in Education and Development, and in particular its Director, Adam Curle, whose friendship I have valued as deeply as his professional help. All these people have read sections of the manuscript, and I am grateful to them for saving me from some of my errors of fact and judgment; they are in no way responsible for those that remain.

Ann Orlov gently bullied me into turning a long article into a short book; Susan Hayward struggled with my writing and prepared the type-script; Trevor Coombe helped me with the proofs and was responsible for the index. I am most appreciative of their aid.

My wife was at every stage a firm and kindly critic, but continued to believe that it all made sense at moments when even I had my doubts.

C. E. Beeby

Cambridge, Massachusetts
December 6, 1965

CONTENTS

The Quality of Education
in Developing Countries

INTRODUCTION

Most EDUCATIONAL THEORIES propounded before World War II, while doubtless retaining their measure of ancient wisdom, seem far removed from the problems of the educational planner in 1966. In the period between the two wars we had discovered that education could be a force in social change, but, except in the totalitarian states, the change of which we spoke was a staid and stately process that bore little resemblance to the kaleidoscopic events in Africa and Asia over the past decade. Few educational theorists or administrators had experience of systems very different from their own, and, for most of us, the greatest leap our thinking had to take was between the traditional schools of Western Europe and the "progressive" schools in the United States. For my part, I lectured for years on education, but cannot recall having made, before 1945, a single reference to the fact that half the world was illiterate. I doubt if I even knew it. It was scarcely to be expected that our philosophies of education would be adequate to cover the problems of the Belgian Congo which became a sovereign state with some 26 college graduates,[1] or of Libya, which opened the first secondary school for its own people in 1948, and which had about 10 percent of adults with schooling of any kind when it achieved independence in 1951.

[1] Barbara A. Yates, "Structural Problems in Education in the Congo (Leopoldville)," *Comparative Education Review* 7:161 (October 1963).

Before we could begin to adjust our thinking to this new dimension in education, we were faced with enough educational problems of our own to tax both our theory and our practice. We had to struggle with the brute problem of numbers resulting from the postwar population explosion, complicated by the growing demand for secondary education for all, which, in every country except the United States, involved a new conception of the relation between primary and secondary education. Sputnik and the threats of the nuclear cold war made us feverishly reassess our education in mathematics and science, and then suffer pangs of conscience about the split between science and the humanities. Forewarnings about automation brought a vision of a world in which the distribution of jobs might be totally different from the one on which the traditional educational "pyramids" were based.

In the meantime, an increasing number of us were concerning ourselves with education in the developing countries, and, in the process, were discovering that many of our cherished beliefs and practices were fit for domestic consumption only and were not of export quality. Painfully we were learning to adapt them to conditions very different from those from which they sprang, and, looking back over a few degrees of latitude at our own school systems, we sometimes saw them in a strange new light. But we were too deeply absorbed in solving practical problems to have time to draw the lessons from our own findings or to encompass the old and the new in a fresh body of theory; we were so busy saving souls that we neglected our theology.

In the midst of all this, the economists discovered education, and a new body of educational theory shot up that had little connection with the traditional lore of the educator. Most educational administrators were, and possibly still are, only vaguely aware of this invasion of their territory, and many of those who were conscious of it were overawed by the statistical panoply of the economists. We were, for that matter, flattered to be given proof of what we ourselves had been rather ineffectually proclaiming in commencement day addresses, that education is not just a form of consumption but a national investment. This was in no sense a profound discovery. Yet it was not until the postwar growth of technology had revealed the inadequacy of our own educational systems and the plight of emergent[2] countries had shown their tragic lack of educated men and women that the economic relation of the educational system to the community it serves became dramatically clear. The genius of the economist lay in seeking a statistical proof of this relation—even if he has not yet found it—and in expressing the idea in the language the man of affairs commonly uses in thinking of other investments. The economist's first gift to the teacher's craft was a new economic respectability.

We were less enchanted with his second discovery, that what we administrators had considered educational planning in the past had been a piecemeal affair only haphazardly related to the country's economic targets, but we had to admit the truth of the charge. To be sure, our failure was not unconnected with the fact that, until comparatively recently, most countries had no declared economic targets, and those that had them rarely consulted the educator about them. Yet the problem was more subtle than this. Working for the most part in fairly affluent societies, where a degree of educational overproduction, or even of wastage, could be tolerated, we

[2] The evolution over the past fifteen years of the terms used to designate this type of country—backward—underdeveloped—economically underdeveloped—developing—emergent—reflects an increasing sensitivity, especially in international organizations, to the feelings of their citizens, as well as an awareness that gross national product is not necessarily a complete index of a country's stage of development. In this study "emergent" and "developing" are used synonymously.

had come to concentrate our educational thinking on the needs of the individual rather than on the economic needs of the country. Though no educator worth his salt could ignore the social and moral obligations to be inculcated by education, it was easier to overlook the claims of an economic system that seemed well able to look after itself. We tried as far as possible to provide varied educational facilities at each level for all who demanded them, but, subject to certain qualifying tests, our main effort to equate educational output with man-power requirements lay in gentle, but sometimes quite effective, guidance. The law of supply and demand was expected to do the rest.

Educational theories built on such practice proved quite insufficient to solve the problems of emergent countries that had no margin for waste in skilled manpower or school places. It so happened that the theories and techniques of the economist fitted the immediate situation better than did those of the educator, so that, from the beginning, the new concept of educational planning was discussed in the language of economics, and it was the economists who took the lead, if not in the field at least in the lecture room. Limited though it was, the experience in planning that the educational administrator had built up over the years constituted all the practical knowledge the world had on the subject, but his theories were not adequate to carry his practice over to the new conditions, and he lost the initiative to the economist.

No responsible educator can regret the invasion of his field by the economist, for, fundamentally, the invader is an ally and not an enemy; but the situation is not without its dangers. Not the least of these is the fact that the training and techniques of the economist fit him to deal more effectively with problems of quantity than with those of quality, with the result that attention has been directed predominantly to the quantitative aspects of educational planning in developing countries, though there are few educational situations that have much meaning if considerations of quality are omitted. The quality of education lies squarely in the domain of the educator, and he will only have himself to blame if he fails to balance the theories of the economist concerning educational planning with theories of his own which no one but he can provide.

That is the central theme of this book. It makes no pretense of propounding an educational theory of planning in emergent countries, but it does suggest an hypothesis, which, if proved, might provide a starting point for a body of genuinely educational theory. Chapter I begins with a brief analysis of the concept of quality in education. Chapter II leads on from this to the relative functions of the economist and the educator in planning, and deals with what may prove to be the economist's third contribution, his impatience with the conservatism of education. Chapter III studies in more depth the causes of this conservatism both in developed and in emergent countries, and begins to look at the special problems that arise when the stimulus to change comes from an educational system at a higher level, the problems, in other words, of technical assistance in education. This necessarily involves a closer study of what is meant by "levels," and Chapter IV digresses to put forward an hypothesis of stages of development through which educational systems must pass. Chapter V deals with the factors that determine the speed at which a system passes through the stages. In the light of this hypothesis, Chapter VI examines a suggestion, now frequently made, that a new "educational technology" might be used to solve the educational problems of many emergent countries with no great increase in cost, and proposes ways in which experiments in this field might be used to test the hypothesis of stages. The final chapter draws from Chapters I–VI certain conclusions concerning the nature of educational planning and the part the educator should play in it.

Except when otherwise stated, the book confines itself to the problems of primary school education. Much of what is said has relevance, no doubt, to education at other levels, but to try to make every statement cover the whole range of schooling would only complicate issues that, even on a narrow front, are already far from simple.

CHAPTER I

THE QUALITY OF EDUCATION

It WAS INEVITABLE that questions of sheer quantity should be the first to emerge as attention was turned, in the postwar years, to the educational systems of developing countries. It was figures and not educational theories that were needed to catch the imagination and make clear to the world the magnitude of the educational problems of Asia, Africa, and Latin America, and it was only to be expected that considerations of quality should play a minor part in the early meetings on the planning of education and in the three great regional conferences organized by UNESCO in Addis Ababa, Karachi, and Santiago de Chile. To say the least, some of our more refined arguments on the goals of education must have seemed a trifle unreal to African Ministers of Education in 1961 when they found themselves responsible for 100,000,000 people unable to read and write;[1] or to the representatives of fifteen Asian countries (not including China), who reported in their area some 87,000,000 children with no educational facilities whatever and a large proportion of the 65,000,000 attending school who had "to be satisfied with a very limited amount of education offered under conditions of great hardship and poverty."[2]

[1] *Conference of African States on the Development of Education in Africa: Final Report,* UNESCO/ED/181 (Paris, 1961), p. 7.

[2] "Report on the Needs of Asia in Primary Education," UNESCO/11C/ PRG/3 (Paris, 1960), p. 5. It was this conference, held in Karachi at the beginning of 1960, which laid down the Karachi Plan referred to in the

At later conferences of these same groups, UNESCO officials did make suggestions for some consideration of the quality of education, but these were smothered beneath a mounting pile of figures. I attended one of these meetings and cannot recall any speaker making more than a passing reference to the quality of schooling. If the published records give a true picture, the other meetings were almost equally absorbed with questions of quantity, though the Asian Ministers at their conference in Tokyo in 1962 showed that they were aware of the dangers of this approach. After making a brief reference to some of the things that might be done to improve quality, they said, "But here we are faced with a dilemma. We are forced to choose between rapid quantitative expansion embodied in the Karachi Plan and required by the right of all to education, and restricting that right, in order to maintain and increase the quality of our educational system, which in itself is a costly undertaking. Faced with this unhappy choice, we fear there may be a danger of some dilution of standards in the short run, and at the first level of education. We fervently hope we can avoid this danger."[3]

following paragraph. It set as the target for Asia "that the rate of expansion [of the school system] reached in the last decade should be doubled, and that every country of this region should provide a system of universal, compulsory and free education of seven years or more within a period of not more than twenty years (1960–1980) which is the optimum period generally accepted for long-term planning for socio-economic development."

[3] *Report of Meeting of Ministers of Education of Asian Member States Participating in the Karachi Plan,* UNESCO/ED/192 (Bangkok: Port Publishing Company, 1962), p. 37. UNESCO took up the point and called an international meeting of experts in Manila in 1964 to study the problem. See "Means of Improving the Quality of Education in Asia: Final Report," UNESCO/ED/208 (Paris, September 1964). Among its many findings, the meeting noted with regret "the decline in many countries of the status of the primary school teacher" since the turn of the century (p. 8), and, in defining the essential elements of a primary education, set an ideal that is firmly opposed to the mere rote memorization common in the schools of many emergent countries (pp. 16–17). These two themes are central to the present study from Chapter III onward.

Their decision to run the risk is understandable. Many of them were members of Governments which were struggling to establish their first long-range development plans, and they must have been acutely aware of how far their school systems fell short of producing the number of skilled workers the economy needed. No less powerful than this, though sometimes less rational, was the growing popular demand for education. During the previous decade, throughout vast areas of the world where the condition of the common people had been static for centuries, the idea had been growing in the minds of responsible parents that their children were not bound on a wheel, but, given the chance, could make better lives for themselves than their parents had done. For us this is a commonplace; for them it was a new discovery, and they were not slow to see that the one condition was that their children must first have education. The passionate desire of common men and women to give their own children a better chance in life gave the demand for education its explosive quality, and made of it a political force that no democratic government could long resist. Since many of the parents were themselves illiterate, the pressure was for more education rather than better education, and it was too much to expect them to be very concerned whether their demand for more primary schools represented the best use that could be made of the country's meager funds for education. Nor can they have been prepared for the educational inflation that rendered graduation from primary school, by the time their children achieved it, no longer sufficient to buy the white-collar jobs for which they had sought it; this only created the demand for still more schools, this time at the secondary level.

If the politicians found it impossible to resist the groundswell of demand for universal primary education even at the expense of a loss in quality, so also did the educator. It is no easy business to stand before the crowd and explain that some of them should defer their claim for education of any sort for their children in order that the quality of other children's education should be improved. It is especially difficult for a man who has devoted his life to the spread of education, and who, whatever his doubts, has no firm evidence that a rapid increase in numbers necessarily involves a drop in quality.

Nor, for that matter, were planners all agreed on what constitutes quality in education, and they certainly had no universally accepted method of measuring it. There is no reason to expect that, in any ultimate sense, men are any more likely to come to an agreement on what constitutes good education than they are on the good life, and, in a book of this size, an attempt to arrive at a definition of "quality" in education would probably do more harm than good. For that matter, one of its underlying themes is that the concept of good education varies, for all practical purposes, with the stage of development of the school system and of the teachers who serve it. Yet the onus is still on anyone who refers to "quality" to describe the limits within which the term will be used, and this may be a good point at which to do so.

For present purposes the quality of education may be thought of at three different levels. (These do not correspond, it may be noted, to the stages of development referred to in the previous paragraph, which are the subject of Chapter IV.) At each level in the ascent, the concept becomes more complex and the chances of agreement slimmer.

At the simplest level is what might be termed the classroom conception of quality, quality as seen by an inspector of schools.[4] This obviously embraces such measurable skills as

___

[4] The term "inspector of schools" is uncommon in the United States, where it tends to have a pejorative flavor. "Supervisor" is used instead and is intended to convey an impression of professional leadership rather than authority. This distinction is not, in fact, as great as is sometimes assumed, and some countries employ "inspection" to cover practices not very different from "supervision" in the American sense. School inspectors in emer-

ability in the 3 R's, and the acquisition of a given range of facts about history, geography, hygiene, and the like. Less measurable but equally acceptable are habits of industry, tidiness, and accuracy, and attitudes of respect for authority and love of country. One index of a school's success in achieving some of these humble but necessary ends is the speed at which pupils pass through the grades and the number who achieve the final certificate, particularly if this is awarded as the result of an external test. If we could stop at this point, it might be possible to get a consensus on what constitutes quality, but we are already in the shadow of the dissensions that mark the next two levels. When they have finished noting the errors in arithmetic and the mistakes in spelling, even inspectors of schools vary widely in their conception of what is good education. Is it enough by the end of the primary school to have memorized a certain body of facts, or should the child also have been taught to manipulate them, to think about them? And what about habits, if habits they be, of creativity and initiative? Is respect for authority universally a criterion of quality, or should the school also teach the child to challenge it on occasion? (In the American setting such questions sound naïve; in some countries they have, for all practical purposes, never been asked.) At a more sophisticated level, is education still good if it fails to serve the economic goals of the community?

This last question takes us clean outside the classroom and into the marketplace, where the quality of education is measured by its productivity. Nor can the economist, who is the presiding judge at this second level, be satisfied with the

gent countries usually have more direct authority than this, and it will be argued in later chapters that this may be very desirable at some stages in the development of a school system. The terms "inspector" and "inspection" are used in this study with no overtones, and cover supervisory practices at all levels. For a comparative study in this field see, *School Inspection* (Paris and Geneva: UNESCO/International Bureau of Education, 1956).

schoolman's tally of the engineers, scholars, and potential clerks and carpenters he has produced, for they may have been turned out in proportions quite unsuited to the country's needs. He may show an interest in the relation between the "input" and the "output" of the school system as a measure of its immediate productivity and efficiency, but he continues to hanker for a criterion more directly related to the economy. Some have sought this in the comparison of the lifetime earnings of men and women with different grades or types of education; others have tried to estimate the contribution of education to the gross national product.[5] These attempts to measure the quality of education by the rate of return for the money spent on it have not been markedly successful as yet, but our only concern with them at the moment is to show that there may be considerable discrepancies between the schoolmaster's and the economist's judgments of the quality of a school system. (To saddle either of them with the responsibility for such one-sided views is to libel both professions, but the labels are convenient.)

At the third level, where quality is judged by broader social criteria, new sets of values must be taken into account, and clashes of opinion become inevitable. At this level everyone becomes an expert on education, and each of us judges the school system in terms of the final goals we set for ourselves, our children, our tribe, our country. These may vary from military dominance to the salvation of the soul, from the affluent society to the renunciation of worldly goods, from freedom for rugged individualism to subservience to family, tribe, or state. Fortunately for the common school, most parents do not insist that their varied social philosophies be applied with rigid logic in the classroom.

[5] A useful review of the work in this area is given in Theodore W. Schultz, *The Economic Value of Education* (New York and London: Columbia University Press, 1963).

It would be easy to exaggerate the discrepancies that exist among judgments, at each of the three levels, of what constitutes a good education. Anyone can quote instances of educational practices, acceptable enough in the classroom, that are ludicrously inadequate to meet the needs of the economy they pretend to serve, and there are individuals and groups, beautifully educated if prosperity be the sole measure, who serve no known social purpose. But, in the long run, no economy will remain healthy if teachers do a shoddy job in the schools, and in most modern communities the achievement of high social purposes is closely related to economic productivity. In practice, at the lowest level of judgment, people with very different backgrounds and purposes want many of the same things from the schools.

It is in theoretical discussions that this three-tier concept of quality is most likely to cause confusion, for each of us feels most at home on one of the levels, but is not beyond slipping without notice to a different level if too hard-pressed on his own territory. The economist operates most effectively at the second level, but he never knows whether he will find the educator at the level below him, firmly defending the quality of arithmetic and spelling in the schools, or above him at the third level, explaining why the arithmetic periods have been cut in the interests of some higher social purpose. Educators, for their part, will accept the authority of the economist at level two, but bridle when, in his enthusiasm, he descends to level one to suggest ways of improving the productivity of the classroom.

In the chapters that follow, I shall, as far as possible, stay at the first level, and use the term "quality of education" in the classroom sense. I do so through no lack of appreciation that the really important judgments about education are made at the two higher levels, but only because it is at the classroom level that the greatest measure of agreement on quality will be found. Since one purpose of the book is to explain the educator to the economist and the two of them to the interested layman, it is important not to begin in realms where they are likely to disagree. For that matter, most of the points I want to make about education in emergent countries can be handled quite adequately at the classroom level. So, unless I specify otherwise, whenever there is a reference to the quantity and quality of education, the terms are used as they would be by an intelligent, cultured, and sympathetic inspector of schools in conversation with a school principal at the end of an inspection visit.

This, of course, is too simple a solution to be entirely satisfactory. John Gardner has pointed out in another connection[6] that the idea of excellence in any school depends on the goals it sets itself, but, as I have already suggested, these goals are in turn dependent on what the teachers in the school are capable of accomplishing. It would be unfair to set for teachers in some poverty-stricken African school, themselves with nothing more than a primary school education, the same goals that one would set for trained college graduates in a primary school in a rich American suburb. As he moved from one to the other, our inspector of schools would have to change his ideas on quality; in the process he might metamorphose from an inspector to a supervisor. I make no pretense that the term quality of education will always be used in exactly the same sense, but I shall try to indicate when the meaning changes, and shall not let it range beyond the limits proper to an inspector of schools, interested primarily in the classroom but not unconscious of the demands made on the school by a wider society.

As more has been learned about the educational problems of emergent countries, it has become increasingly obvious that quality and quantity in education are inextricably intertwined,

[6] John W. Gardner, *Excellence: Can We Be Equal and Excellent Too?* (New York: Harper & Row, 1961), ch. iv.

and that the relation is a complex one. Sometimes, as the Asian Ministers of Education feared, the rapid expansion of school systems has been achieved by taking on less qualified teachers with a consequent drop in the quality of work in the schools. But it is by no means certain that the increase in the total number of pupils in the schools will result in a corresponding increase in the number of useful graduates who will emerge from each level of the school system, because any fall in the quality of the work may be expected to increase the number of failures and dropouts.

It is by now common knowledge that the rate of pupil-wastage[7] in the schools of many emergent countries is distressingly high, and a brief study of this phenomenon may give substance to a rather arid discussion of the nature of quality and quantity in education. Unfortunately, most of the figures usually quoted to show the extent of pupil-wastage are suspect on technical grounds.[8] It is rare to find an underdeveloped country where the statistics available are sufficient for genuine wastage rates to be established. The result is that investigators who are meticulous in other spheres will accept as an index of wastage the relation between the population of Grade I and the population, at the same moment, of Grade IV or Grade VI, a figure that is obviously deceptive when, as so frequently happens, the number of children entering Grade I is rapidly increasing year by year. Even an index based on the comparison of the dwindling numbers of a grade cohort over a period of years does not, in itself, allow the vital distinction to

---

[7] "Wastage" and related terms are used here in the sense employed by UNESCO in *World Survey of Education: II Primary Education* (Paris, 1958), p. 21: "dropping out" (failing to complete a course) and "repetition" (spending more than one year in the same grade on the same work) combine to produce "wastage" of pupils. For reasons given in the text, this is an arbitrary use of the term for statistical purposes, and may include children upon whom schooling has not, in any ultimate sense, been wasted.

[8] A sophisticated treatment of this whole subject will be found in Russell G. Davis, *Planning Human Resource Development: Models and Schemata,* (Chicago: Rand McNally, in press).

be made between "dropouts" and "repeaters." From the point of view of real wastage, there is a world of difference between a child who drops out at the end of Grade I before he has learned to read and write and one who repeats Grade I but finishes the course. What is more, we have no hard evidence to show what is the minimum period of schooling necessary to establish basic literacy. This is usually assumed to be about four years, but it obviously depends on the quality of the teaching and on the opportunities the school leaver will have to practice his barely-won skills in the adult community.

In spite of the lack of firm figures, there can be little doubt, on the evidence of people responsible for the schools in emergent countries, that the rate of flow of children through the schools is often sluggish in the extreme, and that the number of dropouts can be startling. At a regional meeting the Latin American Ministers estimated that only 17 percent of the children who start in their primary schools remain to the end of the cycle, and that nearly half of them drop out between the first and the third years.[9] The Asian Ministers complained of a "considerable wastage of educational and financial effort through large-scale retardation and failure at almost all stages of school education and premature withdrawal of children from schools."[10] (A conference held some years earlier had reported that "about half the children attending school are found in the two lowest grades.")[11] In Africa, it was estimated that "of every 100 children who enter the primary school . . . only about 40 complete the course."[12] Such figures as I have been able to cull from UNESCO's *World Survey of Education* and other official reports, though often subject to

[9] "Conference on Education and Economic and Social Development in Latin America: Provisional Report," UN Economic and Social Council, UNESCO/ED/CEDES/37 (Paris, March 1962), pp. 35–36.

[10] *Report of Ministers of Education of Asian Member States*, p. 18.

[11] *Compulsory Education in South Asia and the Pacific: Report of the Bombay Conference, December 1952* (UNESCO: Paris, 1954), p. 19.

[12] "Current Educational Budgeting in Relation to the Goals of Addis Ababa," UNESCO/ED/MIN/IV (Paris, March 1962), p. 3.

the reservations mentioned earlier, tend to bear out the existence of wastages of these magnitudes in many areas. More simply and dramatically, Elliot Berg has recently calculated that, "in the Ivory Coast, it required 26 pupil years of instruction to produce one primary school graduate."[13]

We have even less hard evidence on the causes of this wastage than we have on its exact extent, but experienced educators who know these areas seem to agree that poor teaching must take a large share of the blame. Poverty, ill-health, irregular attendance, parental apathy, and the demand for child labor are doubtless all contributing causes, but both parents and children will be willing to make sacrifices for a good education that they would not contemplate for a schooling that leads only to boredom and stagnation. If, in fact, poor teaching is a major cause of wastages of this magnitude, there does seem to be ample room for planning some reform of the primary schools without running too soon into difficulties caused by sophisticated disagreements on the concept of quality. There may still be differences of opinion on such policy issues as the extension of primary education or its closer adaptation to life on the land, but everyone would agree on the need for helping the schools, by one means or another, to achieve more effectively the modest, schoolmaster's aims they already profess.

[13] Elliot J. Berg, "Education and Manpower in Senegal, Guinea and the Ivory Coast," in Frederick Harbison and Charles A. Myers, eds., *Manpower and Education: Country Studies in Economic Development* (New York: McGraw-Hill, 1965), ch. viii, p. 261. Lest figures such as these should be too discouraging, it is fitting to recall that, even in our own countries, we do not have to go back very far until we find statistics remotely comparable. Writing about city schools around 1907, Ayres said, "In Quincy, Massachusetts, of every hundred children who start in the first grade eighty-two continue to the final grade. In Camden, New Jersey, of every hundred who start, only seventeen finish. The other eighty-three fall by the wayside. The general tendency of American cities is to carry all of their children through the fifth grade, to take one half of them to the eighth grade and one in ten through the high school." Leonard P. Ayres, *Laggards in Our Schools: A Study of Retardation and Elimination in City School Systems* (New York: Charities Publication Committee, 1909), p. 4.

CHAPTER II

ECONOMIST AND EDUCATOR

THE NEED TO ADVISE developing countries on the planning of their educational systems has brought together two professions which, until recently, have eyed each other with suspicion from afar, as befitted the representatives (according to choice) of Mammon and of God, of "hard" and of "soft" social philosophies. For the most part, the economist and the educator have hitherto shared neither basic assumptions nor immediate aims, neither their vocabularies, nor, with the exception of some statistical method, their techniques. Now, with little practical experience of working together on even simple tasks, they find themselves joined in a partnership to attack one of the most complicated of all social problems, the planning of a country's whole educational system as an integral part of its economy. Up to now, the partnership has worked unexpectedly smoothly, due in part to the economic sophistication of the small groups of professional educators directly involved, and in part to the fact that the great majority of experienced educational administrators in developed countries have been by-passed by the new planning movement and have felt no call to claim a place in it. The cooperation at both the theoretical and the professional levels, though friendly, has been relatively superficial, and the new partnership remains brittle and uneasy.

There would seem to be two reasons for this. In the first place, it is the economist who has just discovered education, and not the educator who has discovered economics. The economist, as we have seen, came into the field just at the moment when the world's educational problems were predominantly numerical ones, and, since his professional instruments were devised to deal with just this kind of situation, he immediately felt at home. It would be quite unfair to imply that the economist has no interest in the quality of education. As parent and citizen he is no less concerned with quality of schooling than is the educator, and, even in his professional capacity, he has no wish to ignore it, though he may find it difficult to manipulate if it cannot be measured.[1] It is natural that, in his probings into education, the economist should ask the kinds of question an economist can answer. They are mostly questions of quantity, and because of his training and detachment, he feels no discomfort in discussing them in purely quantitative terms. Despite a haunting sense of unreality in a familiar world, the educator has tended to go along with the economist, and has refrained, too long I think, from asking the kinds of question about planning that only an educator can answer. Experience has taught him that quality is of the very essence of most educational problems, and he will become increasingly unhappy in the new partnership unless questions of quality play a bigger part in discussions of educational planning than they have done in the past. Fortunately, there are signs that both sides are becoming aware that it is neither theoretically nor practically possible to separate quality and quantity in attacking the educational problems of emergent countries.

Pupil wastage is a case in point. Wastages of the magnitude described in Chapter I are clearly of major significance to the

---

[1] John Vaizey expresses this well in the introduction to *The Economics of Education:* "I have tried as well to satisfy the plea to pay attention to the 'immeasurable' benefits of education, though I must confess to an instinctive conviction that what cannot be measured may not exist" (London: Faber and Faber, 1962), p. 14. Some of the qualitative products of education can, of course, be measured (they are the main concern of this book), but others, and not the least important, still elude us.

planner, either economist or educator. Whether he be fore-casting the supply of educated manpower or the school en-rollments and consequent costs over a long planning period, he must either accept the present slow rate of flow through the schools as his basis, or arbitrarily choose a different one. For lack of any firm alternative, some manpower specialists will fix on the existing rate, though few, perhaps, would be as fatalistic about it as John Vaizey might appear to be when he says, ". . . there are relations almost mathematically deter-mined between one level of education and another. For ex-ample, of every hundred children who go into a primary school, it is possible to predict, with more or less accuracy, how many graduates will emerge. Therefore, if you want X graduates, you will be able to argue back to the level of primary school places."[2] In a sense this is true, but no one, least of all an economist, would suggest in practice that, if you wanted to double the number of college graduates, you would double the number of primary school entrants regardless of the vast wast-age "en route." The alternative open to the planner is less absurd but more uncertain. He must assume that, within his planning period, the rate of flow through the schools will im-prove by a fixed percentage,[3] but, while he remains at the

[2] John Vaizey, "The Role of Education in Economic Development," in Herbert S. Parnes, ed., *Planning Education for Economic and Social De-velopment*, OECD Mediterranean Regional Project (Paris, 1963), p. 47.

[3] UNESCO took this line in a paper prepared for the meeting of Ministers of Education participating in the implementation of the Addis Ababa Plan. One of its purposes was to set up a 20-year target for Tropical Africa in the form of an educational pyramid. After referring to the fact, already quoted, that only 40 percent of the entrants ever complete a primary school course, it went on to say, "It is assumed that intensive efforts would be made and that this wastage would be greatly reduced. It is thus anticipated that out of every 100 children who enter the primary school, 80 children will finally complete the primary course." "Current Educational Budgeting in Relation to the Goals of Addis Ababa," UNESCO/ED/MIN/IV (Paris, March 1962) p. 3. The second stage of the pyramid was built by taking a percentage of these primary graduates as entrants to second-level institu-tions. There can be no objection to the use of such figures for statistical purposes so long as their purely hypothetical character is made clear.

purely quantitative level, this is a mere guess. He cannot know the chances of reducing the high rate of wastage until he understands its causes. A prime cause in most cases is almost certainly the poor quality of the work. It is here that the educator will naturally come into his own as an equal member of the team, for he is the competent authority on the quality of the work, at least as the term is commonly understood in the classroom.

There is, however, a second, and perhaps more serious, barrier to the full cooperation of educator and economist in educational planning; neither has yet learned fully to trust the judgment of the other even when he is operating within his own proper field of competence. This is not surprising. The two fields are near enough together to lack the enchantment of distance but too far apart for either profession easily to appreciate the technical complexities with which the other is struggling. Each sees the other's problems as simpler than they really are. Without the mutual confidence that comes from having worked together for a long period, the educator and the economist have managed to run on roughly parallel lines in the field of educational planning, but there is little sign as yet of the mingling of their disciplines in a joint attack on a common problem.

This shows clearly when they find themselves facing together the intractable problem of a country that needs more schools to lift its economy, and a better economy to afford new schools. Neither economist nor educator can envisage a solution within the field in which he is an expert, and so each turns to the other to produce the rabbit from the hat. The educator still continues secretly to believe that, if the economist really set his mind to it, he could find some hidden source of funds for a purpose so obviously essential as education. This, it will be recalled, was roughly the attitude of the Ashby Commission, which reported on the state of education in

Nigeria in 1960.[4] The economist, on the other hand, while maintaining that his primary interest is not in cutting expenditure on education but in getting the best value for the money spent, strongly suspects that, if the educators could only drop their innate conservatism and come into the twentieth century, they could develop a new "educational technology" that would raise the productivity of the schools and produce better results with little or no rise in costs.

There is some justification from past experience for both points of view. The Ashby Report actually did get more money for education, and most educational administrators can remember occasions, when, by digging in their toes, they wrung a few more dollars from an allegedly empty treasury chest. When a secretary of treasury says firmly that x million dollars is the absolute limit that a country can afford to spend on education, or an economist, more cautiously, advises y million as the optimal expenditure, each is well aware that his decision is based on a series of value judgments that could be challenged on other than economic grounds. Similarly, a perspicacious economist, or a management consultant under his direction, could be relied on to find in any school system some waste of funds and some places where modern techniques merit more consideration than they are currently being given.

In an administrative system dependent on checks and balances, it is right that members of the two professions should jolt each other out of a too facile acceptance of the status quo in areas near their common frontier, but there is a limit to this friendly mistrust when they are called upon to give joint advice to a country other then their own. As economist and

---

[4] "We could have approached this task by calculating what the country can afford to spend on education, and by proposing cautious, modest, and reasonable ways in which the educational system might be improved within the limits of the budget. We have unanimously rejected this approach to our task." *Investment in Education* [Ashby report] (Lagos: Federal Ministry of Education, 1960), p. 3. Although the commission had a distinguished economist as consultant, this statement still smacks of the educator rather than the economist.

educator move more deeply into each other's territory, a point arrives where each must be prepared to accept the other's professional judgment that a particular proposal is, or is not, feasible at a given cost and within a given time. This they will do only when they have a common understanding (if not a common acceptance) of the fundamental assumptions on which such judgments are based, and when each has a more profound appreciation than he has at present of the other's professional problems. This mutual understanding is most likely to come about as a result of years of joint work on specific problems in emergent countries, but it might still be useful for the economist and educator to explain to each other in more general terms the peculiar difficulties they face in their own fields of planning. This will not be easy, for educational planning is at that awkward stage where individual problems cannot be seen clearly for the lack of a coherent body of theory while nearly all generalizations are suspect because conditions vary so greatly from country to country and from one stage of development to another.

Over the past six or seven years the economists have been much more effective than the educators in expounding their views on educational planning, and any educator who takes the trouble to master the "input-output" vocabulary[5] and read the literature can get a fair idea of their current attitudes toward such problems as the limits of educational expenditure in emergent countries and the need for improvements in the productivity of the schools. With one or two partial exceptions, I am not aware of any comparable effort by educators either to question some of the economists' assumptions or to explain

---

[5] Input-output analysis "seeks to determine what can be produced, and the quantity of each intermediate product which must be used up in the production process, given the quantities of available resources and the state of technology," William J. Baumol, *Economic Theory and Systems Analysis* (Englewood Cliffs, N.J.: Prentice-Hall, 1961), p. 299. The educator anxious to meet the economist on his own ground could do worse than to refer to this book, particularly chapter 15.

the peculiar difficulties involved in the reform of an undeveloped school system. One could begin this explanation almost anywhere, but, as an educator, I find it easiest—and safest—to begin at the point where the economists have penetrated most deeply into our territory, to the door of the classroom itself. My purpose is not to embark on a general apologia for the teaching profession but to examine briefly (and I hope not too defensively) one of the commonest criticisms made by economists, that the sheer conservatism of educators and educational systems is one of the barriers to both educational and economic progress in many emergent countries. The point is not whether educational systems are conservative—no school administrator who has tried to introduce reforms could have doubts on the question—but whether they are needlessly conservative. How far is resistance to change due to conservatism for its own sake and how far is it inherent in the very nature of teaching and learning within a school system?

THE ECONOMISTS' COMPLAINT

It would be well to let the economists speak for themselves:

We would mention here two additional factors that, in our opinion, act to retard technical change in education. . . . First, education in general—elementary, secondary, and higher—appears to be quite tradition-bound in methods of instruction and in views toward methods of instruction. In short, there are psychological barriers to change.[6]

For this great industry, education, is basically one of our most conservative industries, not with respect to the affairs of the rest of society, but with respect to its own affairs—its curricula, its salary structure, its folklore. Projections such as Professor Tinbergen's have the effect of shocking us all into a recognition that perhaps we need

[6] Charles S. Benson, *The Economics of Public Education* (Boston: Houghton Mifflin, 1961), p. 469.

as radical approach in education as we have been willing to take in other fields.[7]

. . . one of these [fallacious policy conclusions] is that education is what it always has been and will always remain, that is to say, there is a built-in opposition to change which reinforces the traditionalism of educational systems since one of their main purposes is, in any case, to hand on the tradition . . . I would feel, then, that one of the major tasks of the economist coming into education is to lay emphasis on the importance of developing new techniques in education.[8]

Frederick Harbison presented this theme most strikingly in 1961, at a conference on aid to developing countries:

It is unquestionably true that the cost of primary education must be kept down, otherwise it will consume most of the resources which are more urgently needed for secondary and higher education . . . Consequently developing countries should concentrate their attention on finding new techniques of education which can be utilized effectively by large numbers of teachers who themselves have had little more than a primary education and which can maximize the strategic services of a very small group of more highly trained personnel. The application of new teaching techniques—visual aids, programmed learning, instruction by radio and television, revised and simplified curricula and texts—offer a real challenge both to the developing countries and the assisting countries. The discovery of new techniques for primary education will be given much more serious consideration once it is understood by politicians, planners, educators and outside experts alike that under conditions of accelerated growth it will be impossible to raise substantially either the pay or the qualifications of teachers in the near future.[9]

[7] Philip H. Coombs, speaking as chairman of the *Policy Conference on Economic Growth and Investment in Education: III The Challenge of Aid to Newly Developing Countries* (Paris: OECD, 1962), p. 87. The reference to Tinbergen is to a paper included in the same report: J. Tinbergen and H. C. Bos, "The Global Demand for Higher and Secondary Education in the Underdeveloped Countries in the Next Decade," p. 71.

[8] John Vaizey, "The Role of Education in Economic Development," p. 43.

[9] Frederick H. Harbison, "The Strategy of Human Resource Development in Modernizing Economies," in *Policy Conference on Economic Growth and Investment in Education,* p. 25.

But, he adds rather sadly, "Those who are accustomed to traditional methods of elementary education are suspicious of new techniques." Writing again, in 1964, after further experience in the field, Harbison, with C. A. Myers, reiterates the point with regard to "underdeveloped" and "partially-developed" countries (levels I and II of his four-fold classification of stages of development): "The basic problem, then, is to find new technologies of primary education which can be utilized effectively by low-paid, poorly educated, and unqualified teachers."[10]

ANALYSIS OF THE PROBLEM

In charging educators with conservatism the economists tell us nothing we did not already know, but they do drive us to analyze in greater depth the causes for the conservatism. What we are concerned with here is essentially an examination of our own professional conscience rather than a debate with a sister profession. If it be true that our sheer reluctance to change threatens to slow down the development of some emergent countries, we owe it to them to amend our ways; in so far as rapid change is impossible, we owe it to ourselves to explain why. But it helps to begin with questions set by outsiders, which is the value of the economists' comments quoted above. Professor Harbison's statement is particularly useful as a jumping-off point. In returning to it again and again in the chapters that follow, I may give a casual suggestion more weight than he ever intended it to have, but it is a point of view that is now commonly expressed by other economists and by some educators. Above all, it does raise questions that are concrete and specific enough to demand an equally

[10] Frederick H. Harbison and C. A. Myers, *Education, Manpower and Economic Growth* (New York: McGraw-Hill, 1964), p. 98.

specific reply, and, at the same time, brings to focus principles and conflicting theories that may be more important than the practical suggestion he makes.

At the concrete and practical level two obvious questions present themselves. Are Harbison's suggestions for improving the quality of primary education by new techniques, without increasing the cost, in fact feasible? If so, why have they not been applied, or at least strongly advocated, by more educators? Neither question can be answered without a closer examination of what we mean by feasible. A particular educational technique may fail to be introduced into an area for any of several reasons:

(1) because the teachers do not know about it,

(2) because the necessary equipment and materials are not available or cost too much to install or maintain,

(3) because the pupils in the area do not respond to this particular technique,

(4) because the technique calls for knowledge, understanding, or other qualities that the bulk of the teachers in the area just do not possess,

(5) because teachers and educational administrators are simply conservative and suspicious of new techniques.

With the exception of the first, we know little enough about any of these reasons, but it is the fourth that is most commonly overlooked. We are inclined to assume that, if a pilot project shows that selected teachers can use the technique successfully with sample classes in any area, one can safely plan for making the practice universal. Any opposition can then be attributed to the fifth of the reasons, sheer conservatism. Yet every administrator knows that it is just at this point, where a practice has to spread from the few to the many, that his real problems usually begin. Children are much more adaptable than are those who teach them. J. S. Bruner has taken as a working hypothesis "that any subject can be taught effectively in some intellectually honest form to any child."[11] There is now some basis for his hypothesis, but, administratively speaking, the vital question is, "Can it be taught *by any teacher?*" As new methods percolate down from the liveliest teachers in a system to those in the average or below-average brackets, misunderstanding, incapacity, and simple dreariness can kill the living spark on which success depends.

If, as Harbison suggests, emergent countries will have to rely on the services of a high proportion of "low-paid, poorly educated, and unqualified" teachers, it is important to know if their failure to use techniques we offer them is due to the fact that they do not want to apply them, or that they cannot. If simple conservatism is all we have to contend with, we should be able to devise ways of circumventing it, but, if these new techniques call for knowledge, understanding, or qualities that the average teacher does not possess, the remedy may be tedious and expensive, involving better education, higher qualifications, and consequently higher pay for the service as a whole. Hence the need for a closer analysis of the nature and causes of educational conservatism. The kind of advice we give to the government of a developing country will depend in some measure on the degree to which we judge the conservatism of its teachers to be unjustifiable.

[11] Jerome S. Bruner, *The Process of Education* (Cambridge, Mass.: Harvard University Press, 1961), p. 33.

CHAPTER III

EDUCATIONAL CONSERVATISM

SOCIAL, ECONOMIC, AND ADMINISTRATIVE CAUSES

ONE MUST BEGIN by admitting that education systems are, by nature, conservative. As Adam Curle has said, ". . . in most societies for most of recorded time, education has been a reactionary force rather than a progressive one. Education, often closely associated with religion, has tended rather to hallow antiquity than to promote innovation."[1] Sometimes, after major political or social revolutions, education has been deliberately used to break ancient molds, and frequently the mere spread of education has slowly eroded old systems of values, but most societies have been suspicious of experiments with their children's education, and few more so than those in the emergent and ex-colonial countries.

Parents in these countries often have a clear idea of what constitutes education; it is the kind of academic schooling their European rulers had, which has been handed on to them, perhaps in a watered-down form, through the schools of the missions or of the state. However unfitted it might be to the life of the primitive village or farm, this was the type of education that evidently gave the European his material superiority and that offered the local boy a hope of release from the poverty

---

[1] Adam Curle, "Education, Politics, and Development," *Comparative Education Review* 8:33 (February 1964).

and tedium of life on the land. W. E. F. Ward wrote in 1959, "Hence the anxiety not to deviate at all from the syllabus as devised for the English pupils. Like King Wenceslas's page, our African pupils mark our footsteps and tread in them."[2] A year or two earlier, Christopher Cox, then Educational Adviser to the Secretary of State for the Colonies, said, "The general practice all over British Africa, despite its many remaining backward areas, is today increasingly one on which the Africans have set their hearts, with an impatient fervour that it is hard for us to realize, upon a complete Western education as they believe it to be."[3] Since then, independence, the spirit of nationalism, and increasing contacts with other countries have begun to change this conception at the national and political levels, but the time has been too short for any profound remodeling of school systems, and it is unlikely that the average parent's stereotype of a good education for his children has been greatly modified. Any change to a more realistic and practical form of education better suited to the needs of farm or factory is liable to be regarded as a subtle attempt to fob children off with something inferior. A quarter of a century ago I sat in a Maori village in a remote corner of New Zealand, trying to persuade the chiefs and elders to accept for their district a secondary school providing the technical courses the area so clearly needed rather than the classical course on which they had set their hearts. What they were being offered was, in fact, an expensive type of school for a rural area, but their ideal of an educated man was based on the Oxbridge graduates who had come to New Zealand as missionaries a century before, and neither John Dewey nor an economist with his promise of productivity would have shaken

[2] W. E. F. Ward, *Educating Young Nations* (London: Allen and Unwin, 1959), p. 61.

[3] Christopher Cox, Presidential Address to the Education Section of the British Association for the Advancement of Science, 1956.

them. I retired, defeated, when an old chief, having shrewdly elicited that I had myself taken Latin, clinched the argument with, "And look where you got to!" The proper reply still eludes me.

It is a situation that could be duplicated in many ex-colonial countries. The anthropologist and the educational theorist may be shocked that an educational adviser in such a country should acquiesce in the continuance of a school system so patently devised to serve a very different form of society, and they would have no difficulty in finding in Africa and Asia scores of examples of curricula and educational objectives more suited to England and France half a century ago than to the crying needs of an emergent tropical country today. But, quite apart from the practical difficulties of suddenly changing a school system, which will be considered later, there is the overriding consideration, easily forgotten in our enthusiasm, that the final arbiter of a country's educational goals is the country itself. This does not mean that every village should be free to fix the curriculum of its own school, but the collective demands of parents will carry weight with most governments, even though this may involve the continuance of educational practices that, however much the individual may want them for his own children, are of dubious value to the country and its economy.

Nor can this attitude of parents be dismissed as completely irrational in a country where the opportunities for economic advancement are geared to the conventional, academic system of education. An Asian or African peasant, whose meager patch of ground cannot support all his sons, can scarcely be blamed for seeking for some of them the kind of schooling that will offer hope of escape from the land, and for looking askance at changes of curriculum or method that might bind them more closely to farm or village that can offer them no future. This is one reason why well-intentioned schemes for giving an "agricultural bias" to primary schools have failed with such dismal regularity in most agricultural countries. Similarly, the "basic schools" of India, supported by the government, and strengthened by the Gandhi mystique, have run into parental opposition because they have found difficulty in meshing with the regular secondary schools and universities, whose examination qualifications open up new worlds to the young man in search of employment. Even when, for so many, the hope proves illusory, and a class of unemployed intellectuals results, the demand for an academic education goes on, and opportunities for technical training are shunned in many countries of Asia and Africa. Here again, the cause may lie as much in the structure of the economic and social systems as in the blindness of the individual's demand or in the conservatism of the schools. If society as a whole looks down on any form of manual labor, and if, as so often happens in state services, the starting salary for a young man with the most miserable degree is higher than the top rate for a skilled craftsman or a competent technician,[4] the individual is not entirely senseless who chooses the goal, however narrow, that society obviously values most highly. The schools and colleges that cling to outmoded courses and methods that help him achieve this ambition can at least claim to have the interests of their present pupils at heart and to be giving the public what it wants, even though, in the long run, the community as a whole would be better served by a very different type of institution. The general public, and indeed the state itself, by reason of

[4] For example, as at the moment of writing the minimum starting salary in the Libyan Civil Service for a college graduate of any kind is £900 a year, which is the ceiling for even the most skilled and experienced technicians after years of service. One result is that training courses for technicians, based on a completed secondary education, fail for lack of recruits, although Libya sorely needs technicians. This kind of salary structure is found in many emergent countries.

the demands they make on the schools, must often share with the educator the blame for the conservatism of the system.

The influence of the state and of local authorities on the schools does not cease with the psychological pressures they exercise on teachers or the goals they offer to young people. Lack of money can be as complete a barrier to educational reform as lack of ideas or initiative. To the outsider looking in, it may seem that many changes in classroom procedure and practice could be made with no increase in expenditure. I held this view myself until I was called upon to apply it as an educational administrator, when experience quickly taught me that almost every classroom reform costs money, though it may appear on the surface to be only a simplification of existing practice. Even if no major modifications are called for in school buildings and plant, it is a rare reform that does not involve changes in textbooks and teaching aids, new teachers' guides, extensive in-service training, and the appointment of a corps of supervisors to travel around the schools to iron out misconceptions and keep up the pressure for change.

It may be that a new educational technology will some day show us how to give a better education for less money, but the possibility of this has still to be demonstrated, and, in the meantime, most educational administrators would, I believe, accept as a fundamental law of their craft that *good education costs more than bad.* This is not to say that some expensive education may not be bad, but only that most widespread innovations in education cost money, and that lack of money may be a prime cause of the lack of innovations. Charles Benson, looking at the problem from the viewpoint of an economist, has shown some of the reasons why it is more difficult even in the United States to get money for research and development in education than it is in industry, or even in agriculture: the small size of the units and their isolation from one another, the local resistance to expenditure on education that is not obviously "practical," and the lack of economic pressure for innovation.[5] Not the least of the constraints is the "assumption of guilt" that he finds attached to public expenditure on education, a guilt that may begin to look more like a virtue as economists lay increasing stress on their discovery of education as an essential element in production.

There is a third group of factors contributing to the sluggishness of educational change that are frequently overlooked by the layman, though they loom large in the mind of the administrator intent on innovation. Even if money were no problem and everyone in the system were eager for the change (a highly improbable hypothesis), there is an inevitable time-lag in educational growth which exceeds that in most manufacturing industries, though it may be comparable to what one finds in fruit-growing or livestock breeding. Suppose the change demands a greatly increased supply of teachers with the bachelor's degree; if the position can be met by increasing the number of entrants to secondary school, the "crop" will take at least eight years to mature, while, if the numbers in the primary schools must also be increased, the period may be doubled. This makes no allowance for the time taken to increase the staffs of the institutions producing these additional teachers.

Qualitative changes are hardly less time-consuming. If, for example, a newly independent country wishes to rid itself of the educational vestiges of its colonial days, and tailor a curriculum to its own needs, it cannot do so overnight. New syllabuses must be prepared and new examinations devised. Textbooks must be written concentrating on the history and

[5] Charles S. Benson, *The Economics of Public Education* (Boston: Houghton Mifflin, 1961), particularly chapters 12 and 15. The reference to the "assumption of guilt" is on p. 470. Since Benson wrote this, there has been a marked increase in the Federal funds available for research in education.

geography of Africa rather than of Europe, on the flora and fauna of the tropics instead of the temperate zones. Experience has shown that this is a process that cannot be rushed except at the risk of a serious drop in standards, and money and the years slip away in trial and error, pilot projects and revisions, conferences and evaluation. Then begins the more arduous task of training teachers to use the new instruments and persuading them to discard the old. To the conservatism of parents and administrators is added the conservatism of the profession.

PROFESSIONAL CAUSES OF CONSERVATISM IN ALL COUNTRIES

When one leaves the social, economic, and administrative causes of conservatism to consider the professional causes operating within the school itself, it is convenient to begin with factors that make for conservatism in a school system at almost any level of development, before passing on to factors working with particular intensity in underdeveloped countries. We may take for granted the common conservative influences that bear on all professions, and shall concentrate on a small group of conditions, which, while not necessarily peculiar to education, do exert an unusually strong restraining pressure upon changes within the schools. They are, perhaps, five in number. Stated baldly, they all sound pretty obvious; it is only when you have tried to introduce innovations into the whole of a large school system that you see these five factors as constituting your major problem, compared with which most technical difficulties seem relatively trivial.

(1) *Lack of clear goals.* The ultimate goals of education are less clearly defined than those of most other professions. The engineer, the scientist, the doctor and the priest know better than does the teacher where they are going; their do-

mestic arguments are more likely to be concerned with means than with ends. This is only to be expected. Education lies so close to the conflicting faiths and desires of the community that only the politicians are less likely than the teachers to come to agreement on a common purpose for their craft. Teachers' organizations may, from time to time, arrive at agreed formulas, but the more representative the body, the more vague and general must the pronouncements be if they are to secure the adherence of practitioners who subscribe to very different philosophies of life. A few, too few, adventurous souls take advantage of this uncertainty to experiment, though their range is limited by the centripetal forces in society and in the school system itself. On the other hand, the unadventurous, the stolid, the timid, the unthinking, find in a multiplicity of goals a reason—or an excuse—for sticking to tried and accepted procedures. Unsureness lies at the root of much of the conservatism of education. Boldness in practice springs from a clear view of the goal, even if the vision eventually proves illusory. Education seems fated to suffer from two extremes. In the nineteenth century and the early years of this, the accepted goals of popular education were too clear because they were too narrow, and most teachers were not free to experiment even if they wished; now they are not clear enough, and the same teachers are afraid to leave the trodden path because their goal is hidden in the mist.

(2) *Understanding and acceptance.* Few reforms in the content and method of teaching are of any value until they are understood and willingly accepted by the teachers who are to apply them. In every profession, admittedly, it is desirable that practitioners understand and believe in the methods they are called upon to use, but a young architect or a medical intern, working as a member of a team, may quite effectively apply techniques that run counter to his own judgment. The strength of a roof member or the efficacy of an injection will not be

materially affected by the faith of the man immediately responsible. For the teacher, as for the clergyman, what he achieves is in large measure a function of what he believes, and most administrators will admit that they have changed very little in the work of the classroom merely by issuing instructions to teachers. Understanding, of course, must accompany acceptance; the travesty that can result from the misinterpretation of a reform by a proportion of the teachers can do more to discredit it than does straight opposition. A teacher using a technique that he has accepted but not understood can, by some strange inverted alchemy, turn the most shining idea to lead. No technique seems proof against this.

There is no shortage of evidence of the supreme importance of the attitude of the individual teacher toward a proposed reform. Every educational reformer knows it to his sorrow, and, less directly, experimental evidence tells the same story. Reviewing the results of a large number of experiments on the efficacy of specific teaching methods, Harold F. Clark reached the conclusion that most of them had been invalidated by the fact that the "great dedication, energy, enthusiasm, and competence" of the teacher who champions a reform are liable to have more effect on his pupil's achievements than have the actual pedagogic methods under review.[6] This is not to suggest that teaching methods are irrelevant, but only that good results can be achieved by enthusiastic and able teachers using very different methods, and that the best of methods will fail in the hands of uncomprehending and uninspiring practitioners. The significance of this for educational reform is capital.

(3) *Teachers the product of the system.* A third factor that makes the reform of education peculiarly difficult is that, to a degree that is true of no other profession, teachers are the product of the system in which they work, many of them hav-

[6] Harold F. Clark, *Cost and Quality in Public Education* (Syracuse: Syracuse University Press, 1963), ch. v.

ing spent their whole lives, from the age of six, within it. They tend to embody in themselves the virtues and the defects of the system, and yet it is only through them that it can be reformed. Particularly for the less imaginative teacher, there is always a tendency, when in doubt, to regress to the teaching methods that were practiced upon him as a child. Even when he thinks he is adopting modern methods, the underlying pattern of a lifetime can reduce them to the familiar procedures under another name. Regression to the normal seems to be a characteristic tendency of the teaching profession, and the history of education is strewn with examples of exciting experiments that broke away from the main stream of school practice only to run away into the sand, or, after a decade or two, turn unobtrusively in the old direction. There is no call to be too pessimistic about this. Many of the deviants have eventually had a perceptible effect on the main stream of educational development, but this has never been as rapid or as dramatic as their authors had hoped.

(4) *Isolation of the teacher.* The isolation of the classroom teacher also makes for the slow spread of new teaching methods. Of recent years, team teaching and other devices have begun to break down this isolation in some of the schools in a few highly developed countries, but the great majority of the primary school teachers in the world are shut up with their 30–60 children in a classroom where they practice their art, for the most part, unaided and unseen. The average teacher rarely sees other practitioners teach, and when he is seen in action himself, it is usually for brief periods by an inspector or principal, upon whose judgment of his work his own future promotion may depend. An administrator soon learns how extraordinarily difficult it is for those in final control of a large school system to know just what does go on in most of the classrooms for most of the time. One too easily imagines that new methods, launched from the center with

enthusiasm, have been universally adopted at the periphery, whereas, in many classrooms, they may have been partly or wholly ignored, misunderstood, or recast in the mold of stale practice.

(5) *Range of ability of teachers.* Although, in education as in most human activities, progress takes place because a few able and imaginative individuals are well ahead of the field, there is a very real sense in which the wide variation in the effectiveness and adaptability of the teachers within any large school system is an obstacle to the introduction of educational reforms. Individual differences in the abilities of its members occur in every occupational group, but the problems created by these differences are peculiarly acute in a school system just because of the isolation of the classroom teacher. In a primary school, except for the principal, there is no natural hierarchy arising from the nature of the teaching duties, and a school, unlike a corporation or an administrative agency, has no place that really suits the dreary practitioner wedded to routine. Every teacher shut in a room with a class is, in one sense, as important as any other teacher in any other classroom. If his teaching is dull and uninspiring, there is little anyone can do in the short run to make good his deficiencies.

This means that the administrator, anxious to introduce a new spirit and new methods into a large primary school system, must operate through thousands of classroom teachers all performing similar duties but varying widely in their capacity for adaptation. Changes in curricula, teaching methods, and organization that the best twenty percent of the teachers will seize on with avidity will come too soon for some teachers and too late for others. The educational administrator bent on reform walks a knife-edge. This may not be so obvious in a country like the United States with decentralized control and a high minimum qualification for the teaching profession, though even here it is significant that classroom reforms have tended to spring up in small, prosperous suburban systems and to spread only slowly to the rural areas and the big cities. In centralized national systems, especially in underdeveloped countries where most reforms have to come from the center, the administrator's success or failure may depend on his sensitivity to the kind of demand for change that he can make on teachers at each point in a broad spectrum of ability.

It would be too much to claim that any one of these five factors slowing down the process of reform in a school system is peculiar to education, but there can be few professions where they operate at such intensity, and none where they can be found in such combination and with such mutual reinforcement. For example, if teachers were not isolated, if they worked in hierarchic groups with common responsibilities, it would matter less that their range of ability is so great, that so many of them are vague as to the goals of their craft or fail to grasp the real significance of new methods proposed to them. Again, if teachers were not so deeply conditioned by their own experience as pupils, unsureness and doubt might lead more frequently to experiment with the new rather than regression to the old. This interlocking of factors produces a pattern of resistance to change that is probably unique. It is possible that every profession has its peculiar pattern of "resistance forces,"[7]

[7] To save complicating vocabularies, I have adopted here the term used by the group dynamics school. See R. Lippitt, R. J. Watson, and B. Westley, *The Dynamics of Planned Change* (New York: Harcourt, Brace and World, 1958), pp. 72, 83–89. I am not aware that Lippitt and his colleagues refer to patterns of resistance forces, but it is a concept that seems important in this setting, since an individual resistance force may vary greatly in its effects according to the pattern of forces of which it forms a part in any system. It is possible, for example, that, in some occupations with a more hierarchic structure and a greater percentage of routine jobs than one finds in education, a wide range of ability among their members might constitute a change force pure and simple. In education it acts both as a change force and as a resistance force because of the peculiar relations between the innovating teacher and his peers within a school system.

and that the practitioners of each find their own the toughest. It would be idle to argue the question here, but one thing is sure, that the pattern of resistances in education is complex and closely woven, and that it merits fuller attention by all who set out to reform school systems at home, to say nothing of those who advise educators in countries other than their own.

PROFESSIONAL CAUSES OF CONSERVATISM IN DEVELOPING COUNTRIES

In turning from educational systems in general to those of developing countries, I shall continue to concentrate on strictly professional resistances, and shall ignore, for the moment, the barriers to reform that consultants in any field find, in varying degrees, in many of these countries. Political confusion, nepotism, administrative inefficiency, vested interests and apathy toward social reform are not unknown at any level of economic development, but they tend to loom larger in emergent countries if only because there are fewer resources to waste. When they do occur they exacerbate the resistances within the schools, but they are not primarily our concern here.

One is tempted to say that the five professional resistance forces described in the previous section are all found in an intensified form in an underdeveloped school system, but this would be an oversimplification. Their total effect is usually greater in such a system than in one more advanced, but the pattern in which they operate is different in the two cases.

(1) *Lack of clear goals*. It would not be true to say that the goals of primary education are seen less clearly in an emergent country. On the surface quite the reverse often seems to be the case; because they are so narrow they can be seen more clearly. The acquiring of a few simple skills in the mechanics of the 3 R's and the memorizing of a limited num-

ber of almost unrelated facts are goals that are nothing if not clear. Yet, even if these are the immediate aims of the classroom teacher, it would be doing him a wrong to assume that for him or for the community he serves they encompass all the goals of education. In 1926, Arthur Mayhew wrote: "[India] looks to our schools and colleges for equipment in the struggle for existence; for the secret of happy living, *vivendi causae,* she looks elsewhere."[8] Parents are liable to regard the village school as the place where their children will learn the "foreign" skills that will enable them to compete in a wider community where such skills are becoming increasingly necessary for the earning of a living. It is assumed that family and elders, priest or pastor, and the customs and ceremonies of the village or the tribe will inculcate the deeper values that give life its meaning. Between these values and those embodied in the foreign-born school system there may be inevitable conflict, but it need not become overt so long as the functions of the school are kept relatively superficial and clearly separate from those of the older community organizations. Any tension between the two may be intensified as soon as someone in authority tries to persuade teachers to broaden their objectives, to have some regard for individual differences and for the emotional life of the pupil, and to teach children to think and not merely to memorize. (According to circumstances, the situation may be either simplified or complicated if the village school is in the hands of missionaries.) The consequent complication of goals is not unlike that which developed in educational thinking forty years ago, when an enthusiasm for the education of the "whole child" sometimes led almost to the assumption that the schools were responsible for *all* the education of the child.

(2) *Understanding and acceptance.* A teacher in an emergent country is the first to feel the stress of any inconsistencies

[8] Arthur Mayhew, *The Education of India* (London: Faber and Gwyer, 1926), p. 4.

between the values of the community and those inherent in the school system. He may be expected to teach children to question authority in a society based on acceptance, or to encourage competition and preeminence in a community where, as Margaret Mead has shown in Samoa,[9] these were not traditionally regarded as marks of virtue in the child. It is for the anthropologist rather than the educator to discover how far the clash between two underlying sets of values intensifies the resistance to change in some countries. It is sufficient here to note that the teacher in an emergent country, as soon as he ceases to be satisfied with the simplest of goals for his craft, may find, behind the uncertainties experienced by all teachers, the deeper cleavages between two cultures. Confused and unsure of his goals, unless he is an unusual person he will shy away from innovations that threaten to reduce still further his sense of inner security, and, if he does accept them, he will tend to mold them as closely as possible to familiar practices.

(3) *Teachers the product of the system.* In an emergent country, teachers can be in a very complete sense the product of the schools in which they work. Many of them may have had little more than primary schooling, and some will have had no period of teacher training that could have made them aware of teaching methods more enlightened than those to which they were themselves subjected. Their own education may not have reached the stage at which it is self-supporting in the sense that, by reading and inquiring, they are inclined, or able, to fill in the gaps and extend its boundaries. Even if they are, there may be no library within reach, no newspaper of a standard to enlarge their horizons, and no one in the village to provide intellectual stimulation. Until the authorities can produce new textbooks, teachers' guides, and training courses, such teachers can, with the best will in the world,

9 Margaret Mead, *From the South Seas: Coming of Age in Samoa* (New York: William Morrow, 1939), chs. viii and ix.

teach only what they have been taught. They are the prisoners of their own narrow experience, and the longer they are left within its confines the harder it becomes to set them free. The surprising thing is that, even under these conditions, a few of the liveliest teachers will, with sacrifice and determination, continue to grow professionally.

(4) *Isolation of the teachers.* Because of the nature of tropical architecture and of gross overcrowding, the actual physical isolation of the teacher and his class is sometimes not as complete as it is in advanced countries, but the conditions are such that this proximity is rarely regarded as a boon. Indeed, the fact that two classes are within sight and sound of each other, or are jammed together in one room, may discourage a teacher from trying new methods that involve more activity, threaten to raise the noise-level, or distract the attention of his neighbor's pupils. At the other extreme, the isolation of a village teacher in a one-roomed school may be profound in a poor agricultural country. Even in developed countries educational reforms often lag in rural areas. It must not be assumed, however, that physical isolation is the only, or even the main, factor to be considered. I have known vigorous and experimental teaching to go on in sparsely populated areas where communications were good enough to enable teachers to get together on the weekend, where their professional organization was interested in making opportunities for them to discuss their work, and where the educational authority made special efforts to keep them in touch with modern movements. And there are schools in cities where there is little or no professional dialogue among people teaching in adjoining rooms. It does seem that innovation and experiment in education flourish best when teachers can gain both stimulation and courage from discussion with their fellow teachers. One would expect this to be most intense when teachers are

well-educated and well-trained and have developed a strong sense of profession, but there are ways in which it can be encouraged at humbler levels.

(5) *Range of ability of teachers.* The spread of ability and adaptability within the teaching service of an emergent country may or may not be greater than in a developed one, but the dead-weight of the ill-educated and untrained teachers toward the bottom of the scale hangs heavy on the shoulders of the small proportion eager for change. In a centralized system—as these usually are—curricula, textbooks, teaching methods, inspection systems, and disciplinary regulations must all be adapted to the needs and the limited powers of the average and below-average teachers, and the very measures that are necessary to support and control these will constitute the main barrier to experiment by their livelier and more able colleagues.

More serious than the range of ability within any one teaching service is the gap between the teachers in an emergent country who are being urged to adopt a new teaching method, and the teachers in the advanced system where the technique was developed. The reference here, needless to say, is to differences not of native ability but of general education and professional training. The average primary teacher in the United States is a college graduate, professionally trained. Contrasted with this are two cases, admittedly rather extreme, in Africa. The Ashby Commission, speaking of the primary school teachers in Nigeria, in 1960, reported "a staggering figure of 73 percent with no more than a primary education to prepare the next generation,"[10] and the Minister of Education of Liberia wrote, "Eighty-five percent of our elementary school

---

[10] *Investment in Education* [Ashby Report] (Lagos: Federal Ministry of Education, 1960), p. 81. The situation has considerably improved since then.

teachers are not qualified to teach in the schools."[11] The transplanting of educational practices from one of these levels to the other is a delicate process that can easily go wrong, and that merits more attention than anyone has yet given to it, particularly as it lies at the base of all technical-assistance projects in education.

It has taken advanced countries of the world a hundred years to work out systems of primary education tolerably well adapted to the needs of their communities and to the varied capacities of the children in their schools; today many emergent countries are trying to do the same thing in a decade. At first sight, it might appear that, with our aid and benefiting from our experience, they could leap the century and establish straight away something approaching our good modern type of classroom without having to plod through the stage of dreary formalism that marked the first fifty years of our own systems of compulsory schooling. This theory of the direct transferability of experience is immediately attractive. If it is correct, the main task of those who are advising educators in emergent countries is to teach them how to by-pass the errors of educational theory and practice with which our own past is strewn, in much the same way that many of them have been ushered into the air-age without ever knowing the smoke and dirt of a nineteenth-century railroad system. Professor Harbison's suggestion that poorly educated and unqualified teachers can be given techniques that will markedly improve their practice will be recognized as a special application of this theory.

The opposing theory, toward which I reluctantly lean, is that some of the factors resistant to change operate with special intensity on the narrow bridge which is all that the best

[11] "Report of the Secretary of Public Instruction for September 1st 1958 to October 31st 1959" (Monrovia: Liberia Department of Public Instruction), p. 53.

of technical assistance programs can establish between two educational systems, and that this severely restricts the kinds of skill that can be transmitted. Insofar as this thesis is correct, we may be in danger of wasting a proportion of the great sums now being spent on technical assistance until we come to a better understanding of the pattern of resistance forces acting at the junction where ideas and techniques flow from one school system to another at a different level of development. This necessitates a clearer definition of what is meant by "levels," and it is difficult to take the argument further without pausing to analyze the concept of levels or stages of development as applied to education systems.

CHAPTER IV

AN HYPOTHESIS OF EDUCATIONAL STAGES

THE ECONOMISTS have brought some kind of order into the mass of facts and ideas accumulated about economic development by setting up models of "levels." W. W. Rostow, coming to the subject from the angle of the economic historian, dramatized the "sequence of modernization" by his five "stages of growth," which he categorized under the titles, "the traditional society, the preconditions for take-off, the take-off, the drive to maturity, and the age of high mass-consumption."[1] Harbison and Myers, with a different set of interests, divided seventy-five countries into four "levels of human resource development."[2] These classifications of stages or levels, however they may be criticized in detail, give form and shape to an elusive complex of tendencies and fluid movements. The educator has nothing comparable to offer covering the quality as well as the quantity of education.[3] Harbison and Myers, to be sure, use school and college enrollments as the indices of their levels,

[1] W. W. Rostow, *The Stages of Economic Growth* (London: Cambridge University Press, 1960), p. 4.
[2] F. H. Harbison and C. A. Myers, *Education, Manpower and Economic Growth* (New York: McGraw-Hill, 1964), p. 33.
[3] There is a recent article by an educator on stages: John H. Laska, "The Stages of Educational Development," *Comparative Education Review* 8:251–263 (December 1964). This attempt to classify education systems on the proportions of the relevant age group completing various stages of schooling, interesting though it is, does not affect the argument here, since the author concentrates "on the quantitative problem of 'how much' rather than on the qualitative problem of 'what kind' of education should be provided."

but they are primarily interested in them as leading to a strategy of human resource development. A quite legitimate function within this strategy is to suggest the proportions of educational expenditure that should go to primary, secondary, and higher education respectively, but there is nothing in the model to indicate what changes are, in fact, possible at each level. It cannot, for example, give any aid in dealing with the excessive rate of pupil-wastage at the lower levels, and one has no right to expect this of a model devised for a very different purpose.

If we educators want a model of development that will help us with the problems of quality in education that are our special concern, we must make one for ourselves. The fact that we have not achieved equality with the economists in discussions on educational planning is due, in no small measure, to our failure to bring to the discussions any kind of theoretical framework of our own to match the ones they have created for their purposes. Without this contribution from us the picture will become increasingly lopsided. We are quite as interested as the economist in the quantitative problems of education in emergent countries, and have every reason to be grateful for the concepts he has evolved concerning them, even when they fail to satisfy us completely, but quantity in education is inseparably linked with quality, and nowhere more so than in those emergent countries where money and manpower are wasted in the schools because many of the pupils fail to achieve a level of education that is of even minimal use. So we owe it to the partnership to develop some specifically educational theories concerning the growth of education, some intellectual framework that will encompass the quality no less than the quantity of the product of the schools. As a profession, our knowledge of educational development is extensive, because we, after all, have been responsible for it, but it is discrete, individual, concrete, and scattered throughout the world. Little attempt has been made to pull it together into a body of theory about the growth of educational systems in emergent countries. However useful it may be in its present anecdotal form to teachers who can tap the reservoir of experiences at the right places, it is of limited immediate value to the planner, be he educator or economist, who is concerned with broad strategy.

An hypothesis of stages or levels is the humblest form that a theory of development can take, and it may not even merit the title. It is little more than a clumsy device to enable us to use descriptive terminology in a situation where we have not yet sufficient exact information to express quantitatively the different positions on a continuous scale of development. It may be less important that the model should be fully substantiated than that it should form a basis for further questions and research. The hypothesis that follows, of stages in the growth of a primary educational system, is offered as nothing more ambitious than this. Its virtues are that it is a strictly educational theory, that conclusions of considerable practical significance can be drawn from it, and that some of these can be tested out in the field.

The simplest approach to this hypothesis may be to explain how it arose; since my views on the subject are the result of administrative experience rather than scholarly research, perhaps I may be forgiven for coming to it from an angle unashamedly personal.[4] From 1945 to 1959, I had some responsibility for the educational policies of two countries that were 2000 miles apart in space, and, at the beginning of this

[4] In the statement that follows I have drawn heavily, without benefit of quotation marks, from an earlier article on this theme: C. E. Beeby, "Stages in the Growth of a Primary Education System," *Comparative Education Review* 6:2–11 (June 1962). In the article, three stages of growth were postulated, but the second of them covered such a wide range of school systems that it proved easier here to break it into two, giving four in all.

period, more than half a century apart in time. One school system, modern and well-developed, was in New Zealand. The other was in Western Samoa, which, in 1945, was facing educational problems in some ways similar to those of the elementary schools in the United States and New Zealand in the sixties and seventies of the last century. This was not surprising, but it was a little disconcerting to find myself, without any sense of inconsistency, much less of shame, encouraging in Western Samoa the development of educational practices I spent half a working lifetime trying to discourage in New Zealand. Such inconsistency in practice clearly demanded some justification in terms of theory. This led to the conception of stages of development in the life-history of a primary educational system, stages through which all systems, at least of a certain type, must pass, and which, though they may be shortened, cannot be skipped.

If it be true that there is a recognizable progression in the life-history of most educational systems, and if one stage, with its special characteristics, is a necessary prelude to the stage that follows, there are practical consequences for education in emergent countries that we cannot afford to ignore. It would be absurd to imagine that, in the rough world of practice, either the theory of the direct transferability of educational experience or the less optimistic theory of successive stages of development would prove to be completely correct. But, as an educator inclines toward the one or the other, the kind of advice he will give to a developing country will vary considerably. With whole continents as the field of operation, a wrong and consistent emphasis could be costly in money, wasted effort, and hopes deferred.

Enough has already been said to incur a spate of criticism. The very phrase "stages of development" rouses the suspicion of any social scientist, but I have already made it clear that I regard the stages as nothing more than a first rough-and-ready framework on which can later be built a serious study of a complex process of growth. I have also tried to forestall some of the objections to the assumption that there is a single linear process of growth of an educational system which all countries must follow or want to follow. This assumption is not completely true, and I trust it never will be, but, particularly at the primary school level, the resemblances between the demands made on the school by various countries are very much greater than their differences. For immediate purposes it may not be too serious a distortion of the truth to think of primary educational systems in most emergent countries as moving in one general direction, and to refer to stages as being higher or lower on this scale. The judgment is not so much my own as the judgment of the peoples who are fashioning their systems for themselves on models borrowed from advanced countries.

There are, of course, certain personal value judgments that I would not wish to avoid. In the classification of stages that appears later, I have assumed that teaching with an emphasis on meaning is better than teaching that concentrates on form to the relative neglect of meaning; because of its greater emphasis on meaning, I believe that, by and large and with many individual exceptions, teaching in our own schools in 1966 is better than the teaching was in 1880 or even in 1920. Without this assumption, my conception of stages of development of an educational system makes little sense. But, to save unnecessary argument, I have made no assumption as to the relative values of so-called "traditional" and "progressive" methods of teaching within a modern system. The *formality* of a skilled and scholarly teacher who feels he can best make his meaning clear by an emphasis on the form of his subject matter is a very different thing from the *formalism* of an unskilled and ignorant one who teaches mere symbols with only the vaguest reference to their meaning. It is formalism in this sense that characterizes the schools in many emergent countries, especially the elementary schools which are our concern here. A brief sketch of school conditions in New Zealand and Western Samoa in 1945 might give a sense of reality to what follows. The situation in New Zealand was similar enough to that in the United States and Britain as to need little description. The reform movement of the 1920's, based on the thinking of such men as John Dewey and Percy Nunn, had become, if not the new orthodoxy, at least sufficiently respectable to have profound effects on classroom practice, particularly at the lower end of the primary school. The abolition in 1936 of the last examination barrier to completely open access to secondary schools had left the primary schools free to determine their own ends and their own methods. With the encouragement of the authorities, teachers were reexamining their classroom methods and the content of the curriculum, and, in spite of the usual crop of misunderstandings, by 1945 the primary system as a whole was on the move from a rather narrow, formal education to one with more meaning, intellectually and emotionally, for the individual child.

At the same time in Western Samoa an idealistic local superintendent of education was trying to introduce the new ideas in classroom practice—and was, for the most part, failing, because the schools he was dealing with were not the New Zealand schools of the 1940's but something even more modest than the New Zealand schools of the 1880's. The poorest of them were the pastors' schools run in the villages by Samoan pastors, men with a Grade V or Grade VI education topped off with some theological training. The sole secular task they set themselves was to teach children to read the scriptures and hymns in the vernacular and to write a simple letter. The means at their disposal were usually of the simplest; I remember one whose sole equipment was a bare hut, a few old hymn books, a stout stick and a "horn-book," that apocryphal instrument one had imagined to exist only in old histories of education. The educational process consisted of little but rote memorizing, but, by some miracle of perseverance, the pastors often succeeded in their humble task, and many Samoans learned to read and write in these primitive schools. The early nineteenth-century dame schools at their simplest must have been something like this.[5]

The government schools had more form, but classes could, on occasion, rise to 100 pupils, and the majority of the teachers had only a Grade IV to Grade VI education, though some had a year or so of teacher training in addition. Equipment was supplied on the most meager scale, and the curriculum, while wider than that in the pastors' schools, was expressed in terms too general to be of much immediate use to the teacher. Teaching methods were formal in the extreme, and the connection between symbols and their most elementary meanings was sometimes lost entirely. Tables and strings of words, whose meaning might remain a mystery, were frequently chanted in unison and learned by heart in the hope that their meaning would some day be revealed by repetition. Arithmetical skills such as those involved in papering a rectangular room (the lovely Samoan houses, incidentally, were elliptical and had no walls!) were learned by rote but not necessarily understood, and history and geography were often a medley of facts that had little meaning for either children or teacher, although the superintendent was already beginning to give these subjects more reality with a collection he had made of local legends and historical events. Some

---

[5] "Mrs. Livermore gives a very vivid picture of one school she attended in Boston about 1825. 'The primary schools which received children at the age of four years were very shabby. As I remember them, they were kept, not taught, by elderly and middle-aged dames, who dozed in their chairs, took snuff, drank tea, and often something stronger, from a bottle stowed away in a cupboard.' " Walter H. Small, *Early New England Schools* (Providence: Ginn and Co., 1914), p. 185.

teachers who could make themselves understood in English only in relatively routine situations were teaching English grammar and composition. The few European teachers were engaged in administration, in the training of teachers, or in one or two schools in the capital. The process of education became impossibly slow and dreary; children who came into Grade I (sometimes at twelve years of age) eager to learn, steadily bogged down under the weight of repetition, and, except for the brightest, eventually ceased to make much progress at all even though some might stay at primary school into their late teens.

It was understandable that the local superintendent's gallant attempt to introduce a modern philosophy of education and modern teaching methods should run into endless difficulties, for which no one was to blame. Teachers whose practice was already formless and fumbling were simply not ready for such things as activity methods and sophisticated devices for catering for individual differences—and, it must be admitted, with classes of 60 to 90 children and practically no equipment even teachers better prepared might have been baffled. Specialists from New Zealand were sent out to introduce modern techniques, and were warmly received, but, two or three years after their departure, there was little to show for their efforts but a few bits of apparatus in the classroom cupboards, proud evidence of modernity. Something more drastic, persistent, and relevant to the teachers' mode of thinking was needed to get the school system on the move. At this point, the superintendent retired, and his successor set about establishing first of all a tight, formal system of schooling, in the hopes that something approaching good modern education might be built on it later. A detailed and authoritative syllabus of instruction was produced, and the "Teachers' Monthly Guide" set out for each class, for each day, the major lessons that must be given, and, with no great latitude, the way in which they should be taught. Radio receivers were installed in every room, and key lessons were broadcast each day; teachers were told in the "Guide" what materials to have ready for each radio lesson and were given fairly rigid instructions on how to follow it up themselves. The mythical French inspector who is supposed to have taken out his watch and expressed satisfaction that every pupil in every Grade II in France was at that moment having a lesson on the Eskimo would have found himself in his spiritual home in Western Samoa in 1948.

In spite of some forebodings and pangs of conscience on my part when I first saw the methods in operation, the new system worked. The Samoan teachers took it up with enthusiasm; here at last was something clear and definite that appealed to the formal structure of their lives and of their thinking. The radio lessons were primarily a form of teacher training, and some village teachers heard for the first time a lesson that had structure, that proceeded from a known beginning to a logical end. It gave them a new sense of security; if it was far short of education, it was at least the beginning of efficient schooling.

This was not, of course, the only reform instituted. The Administration rapidly stepped up its expenditure on education. With the help of a few junior grade teachers ("infant mistresses" in the British idiom) sent from New Zealand, a beginning was made with simple modern activity methods in Grades I and II to prepare the way for less formal methods in the higher classes; scholarships were given to take some of the brightest children to New Zealand to finish their schooling and then be trained as teachers under modern conditions; others were given special treatment in "accelerated" schools and classes in Samoa under the best teachers; inspectors and a few promising teachers who might be expected to bridge the gap between the two worlds, were given periods of observation in New Zealand schools, especially in the lower grades;

the entrance qualifications for training college were increased and the course lengthened. Even so, there were obvious dangers in the new scheme, not the least of which was that a grievously oversimplified form of education, conceived only as a transition to something more real, should become an end in itself. The story of how this was avoided and how the Samoan schools moved towards modern practice is too long to tell here. For present purposes the Samoan scene in 1945 serves only as a concrete example of one of the lower stages in the development of an educational system.[6]

If it be true that there are recognizable stages in the development of school systems, the social and professional resistances to change will obviously affect the speed at which any system will pass through the stages, but without closer analysis, this pattern of resistances is not sufficient in itself to explain the existence of the stages. What is at issue here is not the *attitude* toward change of either parents or teachers but the actual *ability* of the teachers to bring about the changes necessary to raise a school system to a higher stage. So it becomes

[6] An interesting account of an even more formal school system at about the same period is given by Malajeta Wodajo, "Post War Reform in Ethiopian Education," *Comparative Education Review* 3:24–25 (February 1959). In the Church schools that dominated Ethiopian education up till the Italo-Ethiopian War of 1935–36, the child was first of all drilled in the 210 symbols of the Ethiopian alphabet. He then practiced his reading on a text from the first Epistle of St. John. "He does so by first counting each letter; then counting the letters at a faster speed; third, chanting the text in a slow and rhythmic fashion; and finally reading it aloud and fast." He then goes on to read the Acts of the Apostles, the Gospels, and the Psalms. "As can be seen from the forthcoming description, the 'curriculum' of the so-called ordinary level emphasized the role of rote memory. There is hardly any place for understanding or for the cultivation of a creative and imaginative mind; all the texts are in Ge'ez [the classical language now used only in the Ethiopian Orthodox Church] and hence are meaningless for the child (and at times even for the teacher). The pupil, having completed this stage is able to read (though not necessarily understand) Ge'ez and Amharic texts, and he can also, with some difficulty, write the Ethiopian script."

necessary to examine, under a higher magnification, the resistance force already studied superficially in Chapter III under the heading "range of ability of teachers." At the risk of repetition, it cannot be too strongly stressed that the concept of stages of development in educational systems is in no sense based on the assumption of the intellectual inferiority of either the teachers or the children of any race or national group. People in isolated, underdeveloped, and partly illiterate areas have their concept of education limited by their narrow experience, but there is no evidence whatever that innate differences of intelligence affect the issue. My thesis is that there are two strictly professional factors that determine the ability (as distinct from the willingness) of an educational system to move from one stage to a higher one. They are: (a) the level of general education of the teachers in the system, and (b) the amount and kind of training they have received. The four stages that follow are based directly on these two factors, as will be seen from the chart on page 72 which sets out the stages schematically.

I. *Dame School Stage.* Stage I, which, for want of a better title, can be called the "dame school" stage, corresponds to what existed in the pastors' schools and some of the village schools in Western Samoa in 1945. (Many classes in village schools and all in Apia, the capital, had reached stage II.) At the dame school stage, the bulk of the teachers are ill-educated and are either untrained or have had only the sketchiest training.[7] The syllabus is vague and skimpy, and teachers fall back on the very narrow subject content they remember from their

---

[7] "School dames in England and later in the American Colonies, and on the continent of Europe teachers who were more sextons, choristers, beadles, bell-ringers, grave-diggers, shoemakers, tailors, barbers, pensioners, and invalids than teachers, too often formed the teaching body for the elementary vernacular school." Edward P. Cubberly, *The History of Education* (Boston: Houghton Mifflin, 1920) p. 446. In fairness, it should be noted that a few dame schools, run by educated women, achieved quite good standards.

own school days. It consists of little but completely mechanical drill on the 3 R's, and the memorizing of relatively meaningless symbols occupies most of the time. The teacher's confusion and uncertainty spreads to the children, and, after some years of juggling with symbols with little real meaning, all except the brightest children cease to make much progress. Their first impetus takes them as far as the rudimentary skills in reading and figuring, but, beyond this, the slow accumulation of almost meaningless symbols clogs the mind and seals it off against formal schooling, however lively it may remain in the real world outside the school. In a less extreme form, the process of sealing off the mind with half-comprehended symbols may be responsible for waste of educational effort in many places, and is possibly one of the prime causes of pupil wastage.

It might be thought that this dame school stage presents a golden opportunity for catching teachers before they have become perverted by formalistic teaching methods, while they can relate their teaching simply and directly to the practical world they know so well.[8] But the kind of direct and meaningful teaching one finds in a good modern classroom, natural though it may seem, is based on a complex and sophisticated idea of the learning process. Your unsophisticated and untrained teacher turns naturally to formal methods of teaching, and the real weakness of teaching at the dame school stage is that it is *confusedly and inefficiently* formal. It has all the defects of formalism and none of its virtues; it is formalistic in spirit without having form. When the great majority of teachers are at this level, there seems no alternative for the

[8] For example, I received from an experienced and enthusiastic teacher an inquiry about a teaching post in an emergent country. In it he said, "We ourselves have not the spirit of adventure nor the will to try things different from the past. In S___ they have so little to stick with that they might attempt to jump from nothing to the best of the contemporary without traversing the slow route through what has been held to be good."

system as a whole but to impose more form, however much one may deplore formalism as such.

II. *Stage of Formalism.* Stage II is that at which teachers are ill-educated but trained. Advance to stage IV (I ignore for the moment stage III, the stage of transition) would demand teachers who were well-educated and well-trained, but the distance is too great to be covered in one step from the dame school stage. It is a much slower business to gear a whole system to produce large numbers of teachers with a good standard of general education than it is to give the ill-educated products of the schools a couple of years of reasonably good teacher training adapted to their level of personal achievement. Yet it is vain to expect such methods to produce, in general, anything more than good teachers of a formalistic type; with a few exceptions, their teaching will always bear the marks of their own inadequate education.

The essential condition of good, active, pupil-oriented teaching is that the teacher must have a sense of inner security. (It is curious that a generation of educational theorists who have given so much thought to the child's need for a sense of inner security should have paid scant attention to the same need in the teaching profession.) Granted that, at any stage, he must have the personal qualities that enable him to control his class, at the highest stage he must also have a wide enough knowledge of his subject matter and of its adjacent fields to follow without fear if the interests of his pupils take him and them beyond the beaten track. In the exhilarating moments when, as in some new field of nature study or local history, he is learning with the class, he must still feel intellectually sure enough to admit his ignorance, and deliberately use it as a teaching aid. Except for the "born teacher," or for the deplorable pedagogue whose assurance is based on an ignorance too profound to be shaken, this sense of security comes only when the gap in general education between teacher and class is wide enough.

The teacher in a village school who has himself struggled only to a doubtful Grade VI or Grade VII level is always teaching to the limits of his knowledge. He clings desperately to the official syllabus, and the tighter it is the safer he feels. Beyond the pasteboard covers of the one official textbook lies the dark void where unknown questions lurk. The teacher is afraid of any other questions in the classroom but those he himself asks, for they are the only ones to which he can be sure of knowing the answers. This fact alone throws his teaching methods back into the last century. If the pupils cannot be encouraged to ask their own awkward questions, most of the techniques of the good modern classroom become impossible. Activity methods and childish researches are shunned because they lead all too easily to the brink of the unknown; group methods can be tolerated only if a group leader is satisfied (which in this setting he almost invariably is) to ask the stock questions and accept the stock answers; the simplest things to teach are the 3 R's and a few selected facts that pass for history and geography. The relations between teachers and pupils, however free they may be in the village, are stiff and formal in the classroom; and boredom and huge classes can lead to the tight external discipline some of us remember from our own childhood.

If, at the dame school stage, the connection between symbol and meaning is often lost entirely, at the stage of formalism the symbol usually has a meaning for the children, but it is narrow, restricted, and relatively isolated. Classroom facts and skills are thin disparate things that mesh poorly with one another and hardly at all with the warm, rich world of the child's personal life. There may, on occasion, be a contradiction between the "book knowledge" of the classroom and the knowledge of the outside world; within the school it is the book that wins. I recall seeing a lesson on a fish given on a remote Pacific island. The teacher had copied from a book on to the blackboard a beautifully executed drawing of a fish, but, unfortunately, had managed to draw the scales back to front. This did not deter her from giving, with constant reference to the drawing, the prescribed portion of the lesson on the function of the scales. Although fish formed an important part of the islanders' diet, and the teacher and every child in the room had caught or cooked them for most of their lives, it did not occur to anyone to comment on the difference between the fish on the blackboard and the fish in the lagoon. Facts may commonly be given with more accuracy than this, but, save with the exceptional teachers, the emotional meanings of symbols are ignored, and, even on the so-called intellectual plane, memorizing looms larger than understanding.

The classroom at the stage of formalism looks like this from within. Seen from without, it seems to call for characteristic forms of control; it is highly organized at a routine level, there is a detailed and rigid official syllabus, a restricted number of narrow textbooks, tight external examinations, and a rigorous system of inspection of the work of both pupils and teachers. Teaching methods tend to be reduced to rules, and there may even be insistence on the "one best way" of teaching any subject. This is a description of educational practices in some of our own schools in the years that followed the introduction of compulsory education, and the elderly may find it vaguely reminiscent of their own schooldays.[9]

[9] As late as 1910, Flexner and Bachman, after observing 450 elementary teachers giving some 900 lessons in Maryland, reported on a form of instruction that would appear to have been at the lowest levels of stage III at the best. ". . . the general attitude of most teachers is unsound. They regard it as their main business, after keeping order, to impart to children a prescribed body of facts or information—so much spelling, so much arithmetic, so much geography. The facts are all there in the text-books, and the teachers proceed on the assumption that one fact is as good as another. Whatever is printed on the page is taught without discrimination. Imagine, then, a teacher giving a sixth-grade class of rural children a spelling lesson made up of such words as *Monsieur, connoisseur, sobriquet, sang froid,* and so on. . . . Not a single question was put by the teacher calculated to arouse interest, to compel thought, or to bring out the mean-

III. *Stage of Transition.* I wish I could suggest a more appropriate name for stage III. To people of my generation in developed countries it is the stage through which primary schools have moved—and from which some of them have passed—in our lifetime. So it is natural for us to see it as a stage of transition, although it can easily become an end in itself, the more so since the advance from stage II to stage III can be made by accretions of knowledge and skill without any change in educational philosophy, while the move to stage IV involves the acceptance, overtly or implicitly, of new goals for education. However that may be, stage III does seem to be necessary to provide the conditions for some teachers to break through to the wider conception of education that characterizes stage IV, and so we may call it, optimistically perhaps, the stage of transition.

At stage III teachers are better educated than at stage II, and they are trained. They will, that is to say, have had some secondary education, and may even have completed a secondary course, though not necessarily at a secondary school. It is probable that they will have had their professional training, and even some of their secondary education, in a special training college dominated by what the French call "l'esprit primaire." The gap between what they know and what their pupils know is now greater, so that the teacher feels more

ing of what had been memorized. . . . Thus, in subject after subject, children are expected to acquire facts through memorizing printed pages. Meanwhile, strange though it seems, not half the 400 teachers visited felt that they themselves must know these facts . . . But reviewing and drilling as carried out in most Maryland schools is a cruel and wasteful procedure calculated to kill interest and to destroy the child's capacity for constructive thinking." Abraham Flexner and F. P. Bachman, *Public Education in Maryland—A Report to the Maryland Educational Survey Commission* (New York: The General Education Board, 1916), pp. 106–108. They also reported that, of over 3000 white elementary teachers in the state outside of Baltimore, 12.7 percent had had only an elementary school education, 20.7 percent had spent one or two years in a high school, and less than 5 percent had received a standard normal school training.

secure and can allow the children a little more latitude to ask questions, although it is unlikely he will go out of his way to stimulate them to do so. There will still be fixed textbooks, but this is the stage at which there are probably also sets of "supplementary readers" that will take the children beyond— but not too far beyond—the official texts. There may even be a library of sorts, but it is most unlikely that it will be used, or be capable of being used, as a workshop to which pupils go to satisfy their curiosity or do simple "research." Arithmetic and formal language will be efficiently taught within narrow limits; composition will be as dead as mutton, but the spelling and punctuation will be respectable. History and geography, with the help of better texts, will have expanded a little, but will still consist mostly of memorized strings of facts. Arts and crafts, if they have been introduced, will be taught as stiffly as grammar, but music, for some reason, has more chance of remaining alive in the thin classroom air. The meanings given to symbols are wider than at stage II, but not necessarily warmer. Emotional and aesthetic values still rate low in the classroom, though they may play a bigger part in out-of-school activities such as sports, concerts, and boy-scouting.

External controls, while formidable, are less detailed than at stage II. The official syllabus remains, but is more permissive and the adventurous teachers make forays beyond its bounds; the rest do not. It will probably be left to the school principal to promote children through the grades, though the final certificate marking the satisfactory completion of the primary school course may continue to be given on the results of an examination set by the education authority, and, as the time for this approaches, nonexaminable "frills" tend to be dropped from the day's work.

Few of us can afford to be disdainful of the schools at stage III, for those of an older generation are the products of them, and so are many of the great national figures we have come to revere. Some of our children or grandchildren, in parts of our countries, are still attending schools that can scarcely be classified beyond the upper levels of the stage of transition. The schools toward the top of stage III have very real virtues, not the least of them being that they breed teachers capable of breaking through to stage IV.

IV. *Stage of Meaning.* At stage IV teachers are well-educated and well-trained. Although this is referred to as the stage of meaning, there is no implication that meaning was entirely absent from the earlier stages, or that the connection between symbols and their meanings is firmly established in every modern classroom; yet it does seem true to say that the main characteristic of modern education, whatever its failings, is the attempt to give each child a deeper and wider understanding of the symbols with which he works.

Here one runs into serious difficulties, for in trying to describe stage IV, one finds oneself involved with the current disputes as to what constitutes good modern education. It has been said earlier that the advance from stage III to stage IV presupposes the acceptance of new goals for education, but it may well be that the refusal to accept a new educational philosophy will cause a person to doubt whether the movement from stage III to stage IV represents an "advance" in any real sense of the term. Take an extreme example—an exponent, if one still exists, of the nineteenth-century conception of public elementary schools as institutions for giving a truncated and utilitarian education to the lower orders could still favor the advance to stage III, but he would probably consider the refinements of stage IV unnecessary, if not indeed dangerous, for most of those destined to be hewers of wood and drawers of water.[10] For a second characteristic of stage IV is that the

---

[10] Consider, for example, the tone of Robert Lowe's famous remark in a speech to the House of Commons on July 15, 1867 during the debate on the Reform Bill: It is usually popularized as, "We must educate our mas-

child is encouraged to think for himself, and, except within the narrowest limits, it is a goal that not all societies regard as desirable for all children. This may create in such countries one of the most subtle and pervading resistances to educational change.

Even without going to these extremes, one finds differences of opinion serious enough to make it difficult to give a description of stage IV acceptable to all comers. The progressive may deny that the traditionalist ever takes his school beyond the upper limits of class III, since the pupils spend most of the day firmly fixed in their seats, and show little sign of initiative and creative urges. The traditionalist will reply (and I have heard it done most forcefully by a French inspector-general) that children can be mentally active without stamping around the room, and that, before they indulge their creative urges too freely, they need a knowledge of facts and some disciplined skills; certainly, he will say, it is the business of the school to teach children to think, but the best method of doing so at this stage is to help them sharpen their intellectual tools rather than to encourage the immediate use of blunt instruments on everything that comes to hand.

Any attempt to describe a typical school at stage IV will inevitably reflect something of the writer's personal view on educational goals, but I shall try to make the essential parts of the description neutral enough to be acceptable as criteria

---

ters," but what he is reported as saying is, "I believe it will be absolutely necessary that you should prevail on our future masters to learn their letters", which is something short of a stage IV conception of public education. Lowe made his views even clearer in 1870 during the Commons debate on the Education Bill, which set up the Board of Education, of which he subsequently became the first President: "The lower orders ought to be educated to discharge the duties cast upon them. They should also be educated that they may appreciate and defer to a higher cultivation when they meet it; and the higher classes ought to be educated in a very different manner in order that they may exhibit to the lower classes that high education to which if it were shown them, they would bow down."

for this stage of development. The essence of stage IV, as its name implies, is that meaning and understanding play an increasing part in the pupils' day, and memorizing and drill, while still remaining, become subservient to them. Since passive understanding is thin and narrow, the child is encouraged to build up, by his own mental activity, the intricate web of relations that constitute real meaning; in other words he is taught to think. Unless his thinking is unnaturally circumscribed, it will inevitably lead to his making judgments of values. It is difficult to see how all this can be done with a class of thirty to forty children unless more attention is paid to their individual aptitudes and interests than is common at stages II and III. The subjects of the curriculum may not be very different from those at stage III, but their content will be wider and more varied.

So far the traditionalist and the progressive ought to be able to go together, provided they are allowed to put their own interpretations on the terms employed; but beyond this point there may be a division of opinion. Some educators—and I find myself in their camp—will demand rather more of the school that claims to be at stage IV. For them, increased mental activity and interest in the outside world will almost inevitably lead to more physical activity and exploration on the part of the primary school child than is common at stage III, as well as more opportunity for creative work. They would also find it strange if a school, allegedly at this stage, virtually ignored in the classroom the emotional and aesthetic life of the pupil, as do so many schools at the lower levels. A teacher with these wider goals will, of necessity, adopt a type of classroom discipline that is more relaxed and positive, and his higher level of education and training tends to give him the sense of security that such a change demands. These internal conditions cannot prevail unless the external controls of the school are relaxed; external examinations will either disappear or shrink in importance, and inspection will shade into professional cooperation. The gap between the life of the classroom and the life of the community is reduced. If all these changes are to be brought about, better buildings and more equipment than at stage III seem inevitable. So, in my experience, do increased costs.

The question immediately arises as to where in our scale of stages the primary school systems of America, Britain, France, and the rest of the developed countries should be placed. The answer will depend in part on one's theories of education, but most observers would probably agree that, in each of these countries, there are schools that, by any standards, are firmly planted somewhere in stage IV, many that are in the process of establishing themselves in it, and some that only the kindliest of judges could put beyond the upper levels of stage III. However, the very effort to place one's own schools in one or other of the stages makes it obvious that the facts are far too complicated to allow of a school system as such being pinpointed on a linear scale of development, and that progress from stage to stage is rarely as simple as a neat schematic description might lead one to assume.

CHAPTER V

PROGRESS THROUGH THE STAGES

In the dividing of a process of continuous growth into arbitrary stages, distinctions that should shade off into greys become glaringly black and white. This is obvious when the argument of the previous chapter is stated baldly: there are certain stages of growth through which all school systems must pass; although a system may be helped to speed up its progress, it cannot leapfrog a stage or major portion of a stage because its position on the scale of development is determined by two factors, the level of general education of the teachers, and the amount of training they have received. The purpose of this chapter is to provide some necessary shading without blurring the picture too badly; it will deal also with some of the obstructions to progress through the stages.

STAGE I NOT ESSENTIAL

The first misconception to be avoided concerns stage I. It is not contended that the dame school stage, especially of the rather extreme type described earlier, forms an essential part of the life history of every mass educational system. In many countries, by the time compulsory education is introduced, expatriate teachers, working with a limited number of pupils in mission schools or elsewhere, will have established standards and practices that give the national school system a reasonable degree of form from the beginning. Unless the expansion of the school system is very slow and the proportion of the expatriate teachers is high, it is unlikely that the earlier levels of the stage of formalism can be by-passed. It may even be that a premature attempt to force a system directly from stage II to stage IV can, by removing the external props the average teacher still needs, cause a regression toward formlessness.

EFFECTS OF RANGE OF ABILITIES

The second qualification of the thesis of stages is more far-reaching. To speak of a school system as if all parts of it were at exactly the same stage is an obvious oversimplification. A national system may straddle two, or even three, stages if the achievements of individual pupils, teachers, and grades are taken into consideration.

The range of ability among pupils is too well-known to detain us long. Some individuals will triumph over the worst of systems and achieve a full and rounded education, whether with the help of the schools or in spite of them. Many of the leaders of Africa today came from schools at the stage II level, and men with similar backgrounds were prominent in our own countries earlier in this century. Grateful though we may be for such people, they do not of themselves suffice to justify a similar school system in the twentieth century, when our notions of democracy demand that every child be exposed to at least some elements of the education once reserved for the ruling elite. A school at stage II or III does not qualify for a higher rating just because it produces over the years a few educational sports more representative of stage IV.

The range of ability and adaptability among teachers poses more difficult problems for the educational theorist and the administrator. The term "ability" is used here in a rather special sense to indicate the highest level in the four stages at which a teacher is capable of operating, and "adaptability" covers in addition his willingness to advance to a level beyond that at which he is actually teaching. In the present state of knowledge it is difficult to separate the two entirely, but the emphasis here will be less on the pattern of resistances that make the teacher unwilling to change his practices than on his capacity to change. Small libraries have been written on the individual differences among children, and everything from the organization of school systems to teaching methods has been modified to cater to them, but researches on the effects of the spread of ability in the teaching profession have been disappointingly inconclusive,[1] and, except for purposes of appointment and promotion, the structure of most school systems shows little recognition of the wide differences among teachers. Yet every educational administrator knows that, within a five-mile radius of his office, he could find teaching practices typical of systems thirty years or more apart in time. One man may be teaching at the stage IV level and a colleague in the next street, or the next room, may be only half way through stage III; away in the hinterland there may even be a few teachers just emerging from stage II. These differences tend to be greater in stage IV and the upper levels of stage III than they are in the lower levels of that stage and

---

[1] A review of recent researches in this and related fields will be found in N. L. Gage, ed. *Handbook of Research on Teaching* (Chicago: Rand McNally, 1963), parts II and III. The conclusions are such as to create healthy doubts in the mind of the administrator about the validity of any favorite set of criteria for measuring the ability of teachers or the effectiveness of any particular teaching method, but they are not sufficient to shake his belief that wide differences in ability and effectiveness do exist, and that his day-to-day practice in appointments and promotions must be based on the assumption that, somehow and to some degree, they can be measured or judged. The gross differences in the whole range of practice from stage I to stage IV are obvious enough to the experienced observer; the question for further research is how finely the distinctions can be made and what are the best methods of making them. It may be found that tests and ratings are more reliable and valid at the stage II-III level than at stages III-IV, where most of the research has been done, and where the results are complicated by widely varying views on the goals of education.

STAGES IN THE GROWTH OF A PRIMARY SCHOOL SYSTEM

(1) Stage	(2) Teachers	(3) Characteristics	(4) Distribution of Teachers
I. Dame School	Ill-educated, untrained	Unorganized, relatively meaningless symbols; very narrow subject content— 3 R's; very low standards; memorizing all-important.	
II. Formalism	Ill-educated, trained	Highly organized; symbols with limited meaning; rigid syllabus; emphasis on 3 R's; rigid methods—"one best way"; one textbook; external examinations; inspection stressed; discipline tight and external; memorizing heavily stressed; emotional life largely ignored.	
III. Transition	Better-educated, trained	Roughly same goals as stage II, but more efficiently achieved; more emphasis on meaning, but it is still rather "thin" and formal; syllabus and text-books less restrictive, but teachers hesitate to use greater freedom; final leaving examination often restricts experimentation; little in classroom to cater for emotional and creative life of child.	
IV. Meaning	Well-educated, well-trained	Meaning and understanding stressed; somewhat wider curriculum, variety of content and methods; individual differences catered for; activity methods, problem solving and creativity; internal tests; relaxed and positive discipline; emotional and aesthetic life, as well as intellectual; closer relations with community; better buildings and equipment essential.	

in stage II, where external controls are more restrictive, but at no stage can the administrator or the educational reformer afford to ignore the fact that the teaching practice in different schools may be spread over many degrees of the scale of development.

This is represented schematically in the opposite chart. Columns 1, 2, and 3 of the chart summarize what has already been said about the stages. The line X-Y in column 4 represents the continuous scale of growth from the bottom of stage I to the top of stage IV.[2] B is the position on the scale reached by the average teacher in a given school system at a given time. A-C is the spread along the scale of all the teachers in the system. The letter t represents the number of years over which an attempt is made to reform the system. Q is the point on the scale where the average teacher may be expected to stand at the end of t years, at which time there will still be a spread of teachers between P and R, and P may not have reached the point on the scale where B was at the beginning of the period of reform.

In both emergent and developed countries many mistakes have been made by administrators, bent on necessary reforms, as a result of their failure to recognize that nothing can make the line P-R approximate to a point, that demands can be made on teachers at C that cannot be made on those at A or B. It is possible that, unless the poorer teachers leave the service, the introduction of a teaching reform may even increase the spread between P and R if it enables the best teachers to adopt practices (say at the stage IV level) of

[2] Although it would be misleading to regard this as a time chart, it may be helpful to recall that, in England and New Zealand (I can speak with no authority about America), it has taken about a century for mass primary education to progress from something resembling stage II or the upper stages of stage I to the point that we have reached. Emergent countries should be able, with outside help, to make the journey much more rapidly, but exactly how long it will take no one yet knows.

which the rest are, for intellectual or other reasons, incapable. The presence of able and progressive teachers in a system is, naturally, to be welcomed since they represent the sole hope of getting changes made, but, especially in a centralized system such as one finds in most emergent countries, a wide distribution of ability and adaptability in the teaching service creates peculiarly difficult administrative problems for the reformer.

It would seem that the obvious thing to do in such circumstances would be to give the maximum amount of freedom to all the teachers to teach in the way best suited to their abilities, so that the best of them could sweep forward into stage IV, leaving the others to do a competent job in stage II or at the lower ranges of stage III.[3] Unfortunately, complete freedom is just what the teachers at these lower levels neither need nor, in general, want. In a wealthy and decentralized school system it is perhaps possible to devise alternative sets of conditions for groups of teachers whose needs are incompatible. In an emergent country with no money to spare for expensive variants, this is by no means as simple in practice as it might appear in theory, and official attention is usually centered on someone vaguely thought of as the average teacher. The ultimate skill of the administrator-reformer lies in his sensitivity to the factors (to return to the chart) that determine the maximum acuteness of angle CBQ, which one might call, a trifle portentously, the angle of reform. If the angle is too acute, he gets the reputation of being a radical, and public and press may pull him down; they will probably find enough evidence for the purpose in the muddled practice of teachers who were not ready for the change but attempted

[3] Here, as elsewhere in this section, the reference to stages is to columns (1) and (3) of the chart. Because of constraints or personal qualities not directly related to education and training, a teacher may operate at a lower (or even a higher) stage than would be expected from the description of his qualifications in column (2).

it. If the angle is too near to 90°, the system stagnates and loses its attraction for the livelier spirits. He may be roughly on course when some of the teachers at R consider him well-intentioned but timid, and some at P brand him a theorist (almost the final insult in this setting) and a meddler with proven values in education.

The theory that a sense of intellectual and emotional security is essential to teaching at stage IV and that this in turn depends in part on the gap between what the teacher knows and what the class knows would lead one to expect that the breakthrough to less formalistic methods would occur most easily in grades I and II, where even poorly educated teachers find themselves more secure with the subject matter than they do in the upper school and where they can afford to run the risks that modern teaching involves. This proves to be the case. In Western Samoa, for example, it was possible to establish the beginnings of modern practice in some grades I and II at the same time that more formal teaching methods were being introduced into the higher grades. I have seen Polynesian women—and men too—respond remarkably to in-service training, and go on to teach five- and six-year olds with a skill and sympathy that revealed the born teacher and showed what they might have done with children of any age if their own level of general education had permitted it. I understand from correspondents that something of a revolution in the teaching of the early grades in Kenya has sprung from the Special Centre for English medium teaching at Nairobi. Similar examples can be found elsewhere, but I am not aware of whole school systems where comparable advances toward the stage of meaning have been made by ill-educated teachers of the higher grades. In schools at stage II, where less formal teaching has been introduced into the lower grades, there is, in my experience, a tendency, if external pressure and supervision are relaxed, to regress toward pure formalism, while still retaining some of the gadgetry of more meaningful practice. It is chastening to remember that, in our own systems, activity methods (to use a blanket term for a movement that went much deeper than any mere technique) were introduced into grades I and II a generation before they made much headway in the higher grades, and that, in the beginning, they held their own only because a few determined women had some theory behind their practice.

EFFECTS OF MATERIAL CONDITIONS AND CONTROLS

It would be unrealistic to consider progress through the stages without any reference to material conditions and unenlightened methods of control, which can confine even good teachers to the mechanical routine of stage II. A teacher with fifty to eighty children in a small bare room, with no equipment but a blackboard, a piece of chalk, and a few miserable dog-eared texts, with not enough pencils and pieces of paper to go around, and another class within a yard of his, can scarcely be expected to encourage the unfolding of personalities and the emergence of creative minds. His task is made no easier if the children left home without a decent meal and if many of them are debilitated by tropical diseases. While watching teachers at work under these conditions, I have often been filled with admiration that they produce any results at all, however humble, and that some youngsters struggle through this barren wilderness to real education, but it is important not to let such admiration blind us to the fact that, at no stage, will the majority of children get adequate education unless we give the teachers the necessary tools of their trade. It is easy, in lyrical or economical mood, to dilate on the possibilities of alfresco schooling beneath a tree. Mark Hopkins and his log may be an admirable model for the education of one child by an inspired teacher, but it is too much to expect the administrator to adopt it with enthusiasm when he has a million children on one end of the log and 20,000 teachers, ranging from the brilliant to the dull, sitting on the other. One can find occasional examples, especially at the secondary and university levels, of extravagant buildings that a poor country would have been wiser to avoid, but primary school teachers in many emergent countries work in conditions that make teaching at the stage IV level virtually impossible.

Mental constraints can be no less effective than material ones in slowing down the progress of a school system to a higher stage. Teachers eager for change can be held back by old-fashioned syllabuses, restrictive systems of inspection, and narrow external examinations that have lingered on from some earlier stage when they may have been necessary. Complaints about these practices will be heard in most large systems; they are often justified, but they also provide an excuse for those teachers who have no desire to change their ways. However that may be, the effects of both physical and mental constraints linger on even after they have been removed, and the average teacher can be surprisingly resistant to a new-found reforming zeal in the Ministry of Education. It may take the profession in any country a decade or two to make the most of new buildings, new equipment, and, hardest of all, new freedom.

EFFECTS OF PROFESSIONAL RESISTANCES

So far this chapter has been concerned with the intellectual differences that blur the distinction between the stages, and with the effect these differences and adverse material and administrative conditions can have upon progress through the stages. In addition, when an educational system at one stage of development sets out to give help and advice to a system at a lower stage, certain of the professional resistances described in Chapter III begin to operate in a peculiarly subtle manner. The fifth of these resistance forces, the range of ability among teachers, is the basis of the whole hypothesis of stages, and calls for no further comment. Nor does the fourth, the isolation of the teacher, which operates as a barrier to progress at all stages. The third resistance force arises from the fact that teachers are the product of the system in which they work. In any technical assistance program this can cause a double complication, for there are two groups of teachers, the donors and the recipients of advice, and they are the products of systems at different levels of development. Each tends to take for granted values and objectives that may be foreign to the other. The onus is more clearly on the donor groups to make a conscious adjustment, and above all, to bear in mind that what may be to them only the introduction of a new technique may mean for their opposite numbers the acceptance of a different conception of what constitutes education.

It is the first and second of the resistance forces that cause special problems in the setting of a technical assistance program. While the lack of clear goals and the necessity for each individual teacher to understand and accept every reform can create difficulties for the teachers within any emergent school system, these are further complicated when the movement for reform originates in a school system at a very much higher stage of development. Paradoxically, it was in some ways easier for our countries to blaze a new trail in public education in the nineteenth century than it is for others, who are at the stage where we were then, to follow in our tracks. Our schools lacked both finance and educated and trained teachers, but they did have clear and simple goals. If their practice was only at stage II or III, so also, by and large, were their aims. If they had no one to give them technical assistance with their formidable problems, neither were they confused by glittering goals they had not the means to achieve, nor by a "revolution of expectations" set off by the sight of someone else's riches. So their capacity at any moment was never entirely incommensurate with their discontent.

It must be extremely difficult for the thoughtful teacher in an emergent country to arrive at a unified idea of his craft and of its goals, for, whichever way he turns, he is met by a form of dualism that springs from the juxtaposition of systems at two different levels. On the one hand, he may be torn between the community and tribal values, that give life its deeper meaning, and what to him may be the useful but superficial values inherent in a school system inherited from a colonial power. If he or his superiors have had a chance to travel— and the travel grant is one of the main tools of any technical assistance program—he also risks being dazzled by sophisticated theories, practices, and facilities that were unknown to us a couple of decades ago, and that may or may not be relevant to a school system standing where we stood in 1880. It is not at all uncommon, in requests for technical assistance from emergent countries, for high priority to be given to expensive refinements that are not yet in general practice in advanced countries. It was even more common, in the early days of technical assistance, for donor countries to give to poverty-stricken school systems elaborate equipment that had no relation to any goals they were capable of achieving. I have seen in many schools costly equipment moldering in cupboards while the pupils learned their textbooks by heart.

Whether or not he has traveled abroad, the administrator or teacher from an emergent country will almost certainly suffer in a more or less acute form from the dualism between theory and practice that is, I fear, one of the marks of the teaching profession. In our case, as we struggled up through the lower stages, the gap between the two was limited by the fact that official theory, if not private utopianism, had its beginnings in existing practice and could not go too far beyond it. The educational leader or administrator from an emergent country may now find his theories ready-made, usually to the measure of a school system very different from his own. Unfortunately, theories of what constitutes good education spread more rapidly through the world than does the practice of good teaching. The aims of education expressed in the official documents of Ministries of Education frequently sound very much the same in countries with widely different levels of practice. What the educational reformer is often fighting against is not so much a set of positive beliefs at variance with his own as the passive acceptance of practices that may well conflict with whatever theories have already been instilled into the practitioner. In these conditions, one can produce a change in the theories without necessarily effecting a change in the practices.

The split between theory and practice is widened by the great force with which educational goals and theories coming from an economically advanced country strike the ordinary practicing teacher in an emergent country, particularly if they are endorsed by his own educational hierarchy. The average teacher in an emergent country is generally more susceptible to authority than are his colleagues in advanced countries, and the chances are that he will accept a theory coming from above, whether or not he understands its full significance, and however slight its impact on his practice. If he has been to a training college or a normal school, he will almost certainly have been taught the evils of mere rote learning as the basis of all education, but it is unlikely he will have been given the detailed instructions and techniques for breaking out of the circle when he takes up his first position in a school whose practice is traditionally based on memorizing. For that matter, since training colleges are sometimes the worst offenders in this respect, he may, like most teachers of an older generation in any country, have been taught the aims and ideals of stage IV by lecture and examination methods firmly embedded in stage III. What lingers in his mind is the practice rather than the precept, and it is not surprising that a similar dualism should develop in his own teaching. It is here that some of the newer teaching techniques may have their greatest significance just because they are the result of a conscious attempt to carry theory on the back of prescribed, detailed practice.

This rather sombre concentration on the barriers to progress through the stages might lead one to assume that the average teacher in an emergent country is shut off completely in his classroom and influenced only by regulations, chilly official pronouncements, and occasional awesome visits from an inspector. This sometimes does occur, in which case the poorly educated teacher is not likely to make many changes in conventional practice. Since he lacks the inner resources of the true professional, he is often heavily dependent on support from the outside. In a school system at stage II it is too much to expect this to come from parents and the general public; the most that can be hoped for in the early days of a classroom reform is that they will not oppose it. At this stage, the main pressure for change, if it comes at all, will probably be from the educational authorities, though its effect may be doubled if it has the enthusiastic support of the teachers' own professional organization. The drive for educational reform is most likely to be successful if it is not an isolated phenomenon, but part of a nationwide movement for modernization under a strong national leader. If there is change in the air, if he feels himself carried forward with the rest of his colleagues on a wave of reform, an intelligent teacher may reach a level that previously seemed impossible. If it be true that some of the conservatism of teachers is due to lack of a sense of security with new methods, the knowledge that they are not alone in experimenting, and that the authorities will not penalize them for failures will give them confidence to teach to the limit of their abilities. But if the pressure from the center is too intense, and if the demands made on the teachers are, in fact, beyond the capacity of many of them, the process reverses itself, and the official support that first gave them confidence now saps it. This comes back to the administrator's sensitivity to the "angle of reform" that his school system will tolerate, and nothing is to be gained by repeating the argument. The sole point to be made at the moment is that the proper amount of stimulation from the authorities and from his fellow-teachers, the ready offer of help when he needs it, and a sympathetic appreciation by those above him of both his powers and his limitations will help the teacher to achieve a level of practice higher than that which might be indicated by his meager education and training.

EFFECTS OF EDUCATION AND TRAINING

No study of progress through the stages could be complete without some examination of these two factors—the level of general education of the teacher and his professional training —which, it has been suggested, determine in large measure the capacity of any school system to advance to a higher stage. If it be true that material facilities and methods of administrative control will retard or advance a system as a whole, and that differences of intelligence and personality will cause a spread through many degrees of the scale of teachers with the same amount of formal education and training, can it still be maintained that these two factors constitute the essential mechanism by which a school system can be raised to a higher stage? To answer the question, one must look a little more clearly at the relations between education and training.

In a developed country, as the arguments about J. B. Conant's recommendations on teacher training[4] have shown, the distinction between general education and training is not as obvious as might appear. In an emergent country, and at the primary school level, the situation is less complex, though, even there, a full analysis of the distinction would go beyond the scope of this chapter. It is not a problem to be solved by tight definitions. There is a continuous spectrum stretching from what everyone would agree upon as general education to instruction that is quite clearly professional training. Exactly where the line will be drawn between them depends not only upon the individual making the judgment but also upon the stage of development of the school system and upon the grades at which the trainees in question are going to teach. Knowledge that is quite essential stock-in-trade for the teacher at one level may be thought of rather as part of a teacher's cultural and intellectual background at a different level or in a different setting. Nevertheless, in the developing countries, a useful distinction can be made, in practice if not altogether in theory, between the type of schooling primary teachers share with other educated persons in the community and the special knowledge and skills they are required to learn just because they are teachers. The training college course for young primary teachers in these countries usually includes some element of general education, but, since it occupies only part of a course that, in all, rarely exceeds two or three years, it cannot do a great deal to make up for the lack of a good secondary education. In the case of practicing teachers scattered throughout the country, there is a limit to what can be done to improve the general education of the mass of the profession, though some able and determined individuals, who have reached (to steal a phrase) a level of educational "take-off",

[4] James Bryant Conant, *The Education of American Teachers* (New York: McGraw-Hill, 1964).

can make use of correspondence courses to achieve a respectable standard of formal education. For the rest, all that remains is to provide them, through short-term courses and supervisors' visits, with a measure of professional training in the techniques of their craft.

The effect of an inadequate general education on a teacher's acceptance of new practices operates at two levels, the intellectual and the emotional. For example, a teacher with no more knowledge of science than the snippets he picked up in a poor primary school may simply not have enough familiarity with his subject matter to let go of his few memorized "laws" and disconnected facts and launch himself on to the deep stream of teaching by problem-solving, where heaven knows what new questions may arise. It is possible that a scientifically naïve but otherwise well-educated teacher, backed by such a course as that now being devised by Educational Services Incorporated (ESI)[5] might pick up enough knowledge to get started, and then use his own confessed ignorance to make the problem-solving of the class more real. But the confession of ignorance comes most easily to those with well-stocked minds, and demands a degree of confidence that not all teachers possess in even the most advanced systems. On the surface it might appear easy, in a short intensive course, to give the teacher enough knowledge of the subject he is to teach to enable him to handle ninety-five percent of the questions that are likely to be raised by a class of primary school pupils, but it is here that the emotional effects of a poor education may outweigh the purely intellectual ones. A gen-

[5] Educational Services Incorporated, Watertown, Massachusetts, is a "private, non-profit organization committed to increasing the effectiveness of both the content and the process of education by generating new ideas and by bringing together outstanding scholars and educators to work on course content improvement projects of common concern." It is now engaged in a score of such projects in the sciences, mathematics, social sciences, and engineering sciences, from primary grades through college. Its African Education Program is of special significance to the present study.

eral sense of intellectual insecurity creates an attitude toward teaching for which no hastily acquired and precarious competence in any one subject can ever really compensate.

Experience does seem to show that there is a connection between the primary school teachers' inadequate general education and the type of thin, dreary formalistic schooling found at stage II and the lower levels of stage III. Observers in countries widely varying in ethnic and cultural backgrounds report, with surprising regularity, that the effectiveness of the school systems is sadly reduced because the majority of teachers are satisfied if their pupils acquire a few mechanical skills in reading, writing, and arithmetic, and learn by heart small packets of isolated facts. These complaints from emergent countries in all corners of the world that primary education tends to begin and end with rote memorizing are so consistent that one is led to look for some cause common to all the cases, and most educators would probably agree that the bulk of the blame lies with the low level of education and the inadequate professional training of the teachers.[6] There the agreement stops, just short of the point where it would be of immediate value to the administrator with a limited amount of money to spend on raising the level of the teaching service.

[6] Sociologists or anthropologists would probably point out a third factor common to most of these cases: the classroom at stage II bears many resemblances to the "traditional" society in which it is embedded. ("A traditional society, in short, tends to be custom-bound, hierarchical, prescriptive, and unproductive." Everett G. Hagen, *On the Theory of Social Change* [Homewood, Ill.: Dorsey Press, 1962], p. 56). It is too much, they would say, to expect "innovational" teaching against such a social background. Certainly, the indigenous forms of education in many countries closely reflected the attitudes of traditional society, and it seems likely that these same attitudes have continued to affect teaching practices even in schools modelled on a different pattern. There is scope here for further research, but whatever its outcome, the educator would continue to contend that, of the factors within his control, the education and the training of the teachers are the ones that determine most closely the stage of development of the schools, and that, unless they are improved, there is little hope of advance in classroom practice, whatever changes may occur in the social setting.

In spite of their agreement on the two dominant factors in the case, educators might differ among themselves, and they would certainly differ from some laymen, in the relative weights they would ascribe to each. It is on this issue that policies concerning the reform of education in emergent countries—and to a lesser degree in developed countries—begin to diverge. If you believe that only a very limited professional superstructure can be built on a low-level general education, you will devote your main energies and finances to raising the educational base of the profession, and will accept meanwhile a type of teaching that is far from ideal. If, with some of the economists and subject specialists, you think that the right kind of specific training in the right kind of techniques will enable you quite quickly to raise an adequate structure on a lowly base, you will concentrate on training and techniques, and will find some comfort in the thought that they also contain for the teacher a component of general education. The chances are that you will end by adopting a compromise solution, but the kind of training you give and the results you aim for will still be determined by your view on what can be achieved by training in the absence of a good general education. In the circumstances, it is surprising that so little experimental work has been done on the limitations each level of general education imposes on the kind of training that can be given to the average teacher who has achieved that level. It is the kind of problem that can be put to the test, if not of experiment, at least of controlled observation.

CHAPTER VI

TESTING THE HYPOTHESIS OF STAGES

THE ARGUMENTS I have offered for the hypothesis of stages obviously fall far short of being a rigorous proof. It was based in the first instance on experience in a very small region. Work in other areas of the Pacific, and more superficial observation of schools in developing countries in many parts of the world have given support to the thesis, but as illustrations of principles rather than as proofs. Nevertheless it has been of value in giving a first rough shape to the mass of novel problems involved in technical assistance programs with which I have been concerned. More significant, perhaps, is the fact that, over a period of fifteen years, I found that the hypothesis, first devised to account for the relations between two school systems at different levels, gave a new understanding of the practical problems of diffusing innovations throughout the developed national system for which I was primarily responsible. The fate of nationwide reforms in classroom practice led to the conclusion that only those had a hope of success which were based on the recognition that schools and teachers in the system were not all at the same stage of development. The range was less extreme than it is between countries, and differences of general education were less obviously the main determining factor, but, in essence, the practical problems were those the hypothesis of stages would lead one to expect. It was easy enough to establish almost any practice in pilot schools with able and enthusiastic staffs, but constant adjustments had to be made as it percolated through to teachers who, for one reason or another, were less capable of handling innovations and the ideas embodied in them.

As substantiation of a hypothesis, this is all very personal and pragmatic, and something more stringent is required for any theory that aspires to affect large-scale planning. Proof in any strict sense may have to wait until the stages and sub-stages can be expressed quantitatively, so that the position of a school system on the scale of development can be indicated with more precision. An effort could then be made to match the performance of schools at each stage with the general level of education and the amount of training of the teaching body, and even to experiment with the changes in practice that could be achieved by alterations in these two variables. It would also be necessary to see if the same scale is applicable to school systems, for example in the French ex-colonies, dominated by educational ideas different from the Anglo-American ones on which the hypothesis is primarily based.

This would be a very lengthy process, and, for the present, it may be impossible to establish a positive proof of the hypothesis. It could, however, be relatively easily *disproved* for all practical purposes. In its bluntest form, the thesis is that the majority of teachers in a system at stage II cannot, because of their limited general education, be specifically trained to adopt successfully teaching techniques based on the goals and the modern problem-solving approach characteristic of stage IV. A single substantiated exception, among all the innovations that are being introduced into emergent countries, could disprove the hypothesis, or at least cause it to be greatly modified. What is more important, it might also provide the end of a thread that could lead to cheaper education and to a better theoretical understanding of the process of education in emergent school systems. As far as I am aware, the thread has still to be found.

The exceptions, if they are found, can come from the application of any modern theory or practice of education, and need not be confined to the results of what is commonly called the "new educational technology." Here it becomes necessary to clear up a simple semantic difficulty. The term is borrowed from the economist, who uses "technology" to cover all the ways in which various "inputs" can produce a given "output." For him, obviously, educational technology has no special reference to mechanical equipment in the classroom, but to the man in the street, and even to the economically unsophisticated educator, the term has a strong flavor of the miracles of applied physical science, and they may well misunderstand a plea for improved technology in the school. When the term is used here it has a connotation narrower than the economist gives it but broader than the popular conception; as applied to a classroom, educational technology is taken as equivalent to the sum of techniques of all kinds used by the teacher. Since many of the recent advances in teaching practice have involved the use of special equipment of some kind, the "new" educational technology embraces more physical apparatus than does the "old," but it does not become thereby more of a technology in this sense, or necessarily more applicable to emergent countries than are techniques of longer standing.

Nevertheless, in the treatment that follows, emphasis is laid upon some of these newer techniques, not because they are more glamorous or because they may be expected to replace the best of the techniques by which our own schools were raised toward stage IV, but because, by their very structure, they offer special facilities for testing out the degree of truth in the hypothesis of stages of development. A characteristic of many of the teaching techniques developed over the past ten years is that their goals are so clearly defined and their methods so specifically laid down that their degree of effectiveness in school systems at each stage of development could be measured or at least assessed with tolerable accuracy. So also could any adjustments that needed to be made to fit them to the capacities of the teachers at any stage.

Fortunately, there are projects now under way or in prospect for the application of some of these techniques on a fairly broad front in certain emergent countries. If the experiments are properly devised and evaluated, they may provide information that is sorely needed on the problems involved in applying the techniques to whole school systems. Before these specific projects are considered, there are one or two general points to be made concerning the new educational technology, which may serve to clarify the issues, and also to bring the argument back to Professor Harbison's proposal for its wider use as an economical means of improving primary schooling in countries where the teachers are poorly educated and unqualified.

In advocating the use of the new technology in emergent countries, one must distinguish between the techniques on the one hand, and, on the other, their content and the purposes they are intended to serve. In a school system at stage II the technique itself may be introduced with great effect if it can be adapted to the immediate needs of schools at that level of development, while the content it has acquired in the country of its origin may prove quite unworkable if it is aimed exclusively at goals proper to stage IV. The techniques most commonly thought of as comprising the new educational technology vary greatly in the ease with which they can be adapted to any of the four stages of growth. Radio, television, teaching machines, films, and visual aids generally, can be used effectively at stages II, III, or IV, though the overwhelming majority of the teaching material prepared for use in these media is aimed at the two highest stages and is not necessarily effective at stage II. Team teaching is not a technique of teaching at all, but a method of deploying the teaching force within a school;

as yet, no one knows if it will operate below stage IV or the upper levels of stage III. Programmed instruction is definitely a teaching technique, and, although it seems especially well adapted to straight factual learning, it can be directed, according to choice, at a wide range of educational goals. The same cannot be said of the revisions of curricula and texts in primary mathematics and science that are being carried out in several places. Many of these are firmly based on the problem-solving approach, and their goals are those of stage IV. To be sure, the energy and skill that have gone to produce them could also be used on courses adapted to the narrower aims of schools at stage II and the lower levels of stage III, but the results would be something radically different, because content plays a bigger role than does any predetermined technique in the preparation of most of these courses. In the circumstances, it is not easy to make global statements about the new educational technology that have the same significance for all the items it covers; they are a disparate collection of practices and devices that have not much in common except their purpose of improving instruction. However useful the term "educational technology" may be to the economist, I am inclined to think the educator might have been better off without it for his own professional purposes.

Although, theoretically, most of the newer techniques could be used to achieve goals typical of any of the stages II, III, or IV, they are, in fact, the product of their time, and have mostly, though not exclusively, been used to encourage thinking rather than mere memorizing. The exponent of a new system naturally tends to stress the newness of all elements in it, but anyone familiar with the reform movements in classroom practice over the past forty years knows that what distinguishes the present educational "technologists" from the reformers of the 1920's is not the ends they seek but the more systematic and detailed means they have to offer. The conventional reformers (if this be not a contradiction in terms) of the past half-century have had a hard enough task in leading many of our own schools from stage III to the lower levels of stage IV, and have found even greater difficulty in introducing the schools in emergent countries to a broader conception of the process of education. The vital question now is whether the newer techniques can succeed where the exhortations of the older reformers have failed. Can they, in the hands of poorly educated teachers, carry the whole system through to the stage IV level? How far, in other words, can efficient techniques make possible the acceptance of a new purpose?

As a series of techniques, the new technology would appear, on the face of things, to have much to offer to emergent countries that fits in with their needs and their patterns of thought. Courses such as those produced by Educational Services Incorporated, with their close instructions in the students' texts and their detailed help in the teachers' guides, give the step-by-step guidance that unsure teachers want. The even more controlled procedures of programmed instruction, and their strict formality, seem to offer something of which teachers struggling out of stage II or through the lower levels of stage III stand sorely in need. The method offers also the constant feedback to both programmer and student, which is so necessary at this stage as a reminder, in the language of the 1920's, that telling is not teaching. The techniques that can be classed as media, apart from the vividness they contribute to a subject, can also make possible a fuller use of teachers with skills that are in short supply. So also does team teaching, and it adds, as well, the advantages that come from breaking down the isolation of the classroom teacher.

In the face of such a formidable list of virtues, it might seem captious to reserve one's judgment on the value of the new techniques in developing school systems. There are obvious material and financial difficulties to overcome, but, for the moment, the only point at issue is the limitation placed on the techniques by the qualities of the teachers who are to use them. The question is not whether these techniques are effective, but under what conditions they are effective, with what types of teacher, and for what purposes. Even if any technique in the hands of ill-educated teachers fails to produce teaching of the stage IV type, it may still be of value in helping the system get through to stage III, provided it is deliberately adapted to the achievement of this less ambitious goal.[1] It is an area in which no one can afford to be dogmatic. As far as primary education is concerned, even in advanced countries we are far from knowing the conditions under which each technique is most effective, and, except for techniques of old standing like school broadcasts and the use of new curricula and texts, the world's experience in applying the new educational technology in emergent countries is minimal. Educators who have worked in emergent countries for many years must have a shrewd idea of the uses teachers could make of any technique, but this knowledge is, for the most part, scattered and unorganized. Hence the importance of the more systematic attempts now being made to apply the newer techniques in certain emergent countries. Although few of them are in primary schools, and none, as far as I am aware, has gone far enough to provide definitive results, these experiments would seem to be of supreme importance in the finding of quick answers to some of the questions under consideration.

Of the experiments currently under way or in course of preparation, four have been chosen for mention, not because

[1] It may also be of use in the education and training of the teachers themselves. I am inclined to think that this will be the way in which some of the newer techniques will make their first major impact on the quality of education in emergent countries. They have the double advantage that they can be used to improve the general education of teachers and, at the same time, train them in the presentation of the material to their own pupils. The radio lessons that were used in the schools of Western Samoa nearly two decades ago had their main effect not directly upon the children but upon the teachers, who gained from them the beginnings of a new conception of their craft.

they are necessarily the most important but because they illustrate different aspects of the problem:

(1) *New Curricula and Texts.* Educational Services Incorporated, working in close collaboration with African educators at three workshops held at Entebbe, Uganda, since 1962, has been preparing a new course in mathematics, which already covers the first three years of primary education as well as the first three of secondary. After being tried out by a few selected and specially trained teachers, this course is now being introduced into approximately 500 classes in 10 African countries. An elementary science course, first worked out for American schools, is being adapted to African conditions and will be similarly tried out.[2] A statement of the principles on which the ESI African Education Program is based makes it clear that the special training given to prepare teachers for these courses is to be highly specific, but that the courses themselves turn their back on mere memorizing as an educational goal:

5. Training or retraining of teachers should focus narrowly on the use of the materials they will be using in the classroom, rather than upon the broad range of the subject they will be teaching. (More concretely stated, if we prepare materials for use in teaching elementary science, we wish the teachers to be trained in the use of those materials rather than in "science.")

6. Learning should take place on a "no-holds-barred" basis. The student should be encouraged to rely on more than his textbooks—to use his ears, his nose, his hands, his finger-tips and above all his active inquiring mind.[3]

It is the relation between these two factors that gives the experiment its dramatic significance.

If these courses, as they stand, can be taught in a meaningful way, and within the framework of the ordinary school day,

[2] *Educational Services Incorporated: A Review of Current Programs, 1965* (Watertown, Mass.: ESI, 1965), pp. 43–47.

[3] *ESI Quarterly Report: Summer–Fall 1964* (Watertown, Mass.: ESI, 1964), p. 109.

by a large unselected group of teachers with a primary or a truncated secondary education and a year or two of teacher-training, they could have a profound effect on future educational planning in many countries, and they would certainly necessitate rethinking of the hypothesis of stages of development as it has been propounded. Insofar as the courses fail, in any place, to achieve the high goals set for them because the teachers are unable to apply them, they will face that country with a major policy decision, if it still wants to gain some of the advantages the courses have to offer. It can decide to provide teachers with a longer and better secondary education, using on them, if adequately trained instructors can be found, the techniques they will be required to employ. Unfortunately, this solution is extremely expensive, and is scarcely practicable with most teachers who have been in the service for some years. The alternative may be to amend the technique in such a way as to make fewer demands on those qualities in which the teachers are weakest. In the case of the ESI courses, this will not be simple, but it should not be impossible to create equally well-contrived courses to help the teachers in service to do better the things they are already doing poorly. If the signs are more hopeful, it may be possible to fix a goal midway between what is now being achieved and the best that could be done by the new technique in the hands of more adequately educated teachers.

(2) *Programmed Instruction.* Another broadly based experiment began with UNESCO, which organized two workshops in 1963 in Jordan and Nigeria "to introduce the technique of programmed instructional materials to educators in the Middle East and West Africa."[4] In spite of the enthusiasm of the staff and the participants, they were commendably cautious in their estimate of what immediate contribution pro-

---

[4] P. Kenneth Komoski and E. J. Green, *Programmed Instruction in West Africa and the Arab States,* Educational Studies and Documents, no. 52 (Paris: UNESCO, 1964).

grammed instruction can make to education in these areas. They appeared to see its most obvious application in the education and training of teachers, but, at the other end of the scale, could offer little hope in the near future for printed programs for use in the early elementary grades. It is to be hoped that controlled experiments on the use of programmed instruction in primary schools in Africa will follow from this workshop, and that they will be so devised as to show the limits to which the technique can be pressed in achieving with partially educated teachers a form of education based essentially on understanding and thinking rather than on memorization.

Here again, pilot projects with a few selected teachers will be of only minor interest unless they are precursors to something more extensive. No one doubts that African children can learn by programmed instruction, or that selected African teachers can use the technique in an experimental situation. What we want to know is how much it can achieve with a few hundred unselected teachers working within the framework of a country's ordinary school system. Its failures will be no less important than its successes, and most significant of all will be any adjustments that may prove necessary to fit the courses to the capacity of teachers with different levels of general education. Unless the experiment is planned from the beginning with these objects in view, much of its theoretical, as well as its practical, value will be lost.

(3) *Educational Television.* American Samoa has announced its intention of basing its whole primary school system on instruction by television. "Unlike educational television in other parts of the world," it is reported, "the Samoan system is designed virtually to supplant, instead of to supplement, the teacher in the classroom. The children will receive all their instruction from a television studio, leaving to the teacher the task of maintaining attentiveness and setting tests."[5] The Gov-

[5] "U.S. Samoa Gets Educational TV," article in the *New York Times,* November 19, 1964. The school system in American Samoa, it should be

ernor is said to have given as one of the reasons for this decision: "Teachers supposedly teaching English were incapable
of making themselves understood to me. I could not help but
wonder what the youngsters were learning." This scheme, if it
should be successful, may obviate some of the difficulties of
moving between stages of development, although it obviously
creates a number of new problems because of the minor role
it apparently gives to the classroom teacher. Without an authoritative statement of just what the project involves, it would
be pointless to comment on it further, but as an extreme experiment in the application of the new technology to a complete region, it merits the closest attention from educational
planners, whether it succeeds or fails.

(4) *Team Teaching.* In an ascending—or descending—
scale the three experiments just mentioned make increasing
use of externally prepared materials and lay decreasing stress
on the part to be played by the classroom teacher. An experiment just launched in Barbados is based on very different
premises; it is a pilot project in team teaching under the joint
auspices of the Barbadian Ministry of Education, the University of the West Indies, and Harvard University.[6] The results
here may be harder to assess, since team teaching is not a
method of instruction with well-defined techniques and limited
goals but a method of school organization that probably gets its
greatest effects from the professional ferment that results from
breaking down the isolation of the individual teacher and making him part of a team responsible for its own planning. In the
United States this often seems to stimulate an interest in new
teaching techniques and to give teachers the confidence to
apply them. In emergent countries the educational hierarchy

---

noted, has always been conducted on quite different lines from that in
Western Samoa mentioned in Chapter III.

[6] The project began only in April 1965, and, as at the moment of writing,
nothing has been published about it except some brief notes in the Barbados press.

is usually more authoritarian than in the United States, material conditions limit severely what can be tried,[7] and the average teacher has a thinner educational experience on which to draw. Under these conditions, we have no idea whether team teaching can generate enough impetus, understanding, and confidence to carry a school through to meaningful teaching at the stage IV level, or whether Barbados will, for the present, have to be satisfied with more modest goals in stage III.

The Barbados project is singularly well placed for the observation of the diffusion of any successful methods from the four schools in which the experiment has begun. The island is quite small enough for the first spill-over from the experimental schools to the rest of the schools under the control of the Ministry to be observed with some precision. The University of the West Indies will then concern itself with the spread of the practices to other parts of the Caribbean, and the special interest of the Harvard Graduate School of Education will lie in seeing the significance of the Barbados experiment for emergent countries in other areas with even more difficult educational problems. It is the kind of situation in which no quick answers can be expected.

These four examples do not exhaust the list of crucial experiments being carried out on the use of the newer techniques in the primary schools of developing countries, but the number is not so great that we can afford to treat any of them as isolated attempts to solve specific problems. Nor can we confine our interest to research in the ordinary academic sense of specifically contrived experience. What is called for is some organized method of learning the lessons offered by educa-

[7] For example, in a Massachusetts suburban primary school organized for team teaching the expenditure on teaching materials such as library books, textbooks, paper, pencils, chalks, office supplies, and handwork materials is $30 per pupil per year, which is fairly generous by any standards. In Barbados, the corresponding figure is $.60 (U.S.), and in very many emergent countries it is even less.

tional innovations undertaken in any emergent country for any reason. Teachers and administrators cannot mark time awaiting the results of scholarly researches, and, with or without external aid, they are trying out innovations with no broader interest than to solve the problems immediately facing them. For the most part, both their successes and their failures have only local impact, and the world goes on monotonously making the same errors. Any teacher or administrator in an emergent country who is solving his own educational problem is potentially helping to solve the problems of half the world. Of all the urgent tasks facing technical assistance programs in education, there is none more important than to look at these specific experiences from the point of view of some hypothesis and to construct a body of theory of more general applicability. But the effort will get nowhere without the hypothesis. As a profession educators probably already have many of the answers in their hands; what they lack are the right questions.

The situation calls for more than the collection of a number of isolated successful techniques. Apart from the specific demands made on teachers by the mastering of any one technique, the task of absorbing it into the classroom day may present problems that are no less formidable. In their enthusiasm for new techniques in developed countries, innovators have tended to assume, perhaps with reason, that the orchestration of the old with the new is best left in the hands of the individual teacher. The kind of teacher who has taken up an innovation with skill and enthusiasm may be expected to find ways of integrating it into his daily program. As the new techniques become more widely diffused, it may be found, even in developed countries, that the average and below-average teachers will not be as skilled as their specially selected colleagues in absorbing the new without disrupting the remaining pattern of the old, and it is quite certain that most teachers in emer-

gent countries will demand a degree of detailed guidance that
no one is yet in a position to give.

The group of experts who met to follow up the workshops
in Jordan and Nigeria evidently had this in mind when they
made one of their four key recommendations: "A strategy
meeting on the classroom use of programmed instruction
should be held before any large-scale use of programmes is
planned. This meeting should concern itself with how to train
teachers to make the best use of programmes and themselves
in the classrooms." This opens up a whole new range of questions that must be answered before we can recommend the
wholesale use of some of the newer techniques to make a mas-
sive improvement in the standards of education in the primary
schools of the emergent countries. What is the role of the
ordinary classroom teacher in such a system? If programmed
instruction, radio, television, and films are used by a skilled
and educated teacher to fill a gap here, to relieve him of routine teaching there, and generally to add variety and liveliness
where it is needed, the only problem is to ensure that he has
the adequate tool to hand when he wants it. But if these media
and techniques are to be employed as an alternative to the
giving of more general education to the great body of the profession, the task of defining the role of the teacher is by no
means so simple.

Even the most enthusiastic proponents of a new technique
have rarely suggested that it replace the classroom teacher,
except, perhaps, in the "radiophonic schools" of Colombia
and, to a lesser degree, in the television experiment in American Samoa. The most that has usually been claimed—and that
mainly at the secondary and higher levels—is that some techniques do enable a few teachers who have skills that are in
short supply to spread their influence more widely, though one
is often left in doubt as to the part to be played in the process
by the less qualified teachers. The commonest point of view is
that such devices as programmed instruction, teaching ma-

chines, and television can be used to teach the facts and routine skills that now take up so much of the teacher's time, leaving him free to stimulate and guide the process of discovering, and to answer questions that cannot be resolved in this way or that fall outside the limits of the prepared lesson.[8] This policy runs into difficulties in an emergent country whose schools are at stage II with the primary teachers poorly educated and mostly untrained. Simple facts and routine skills may be their only professional stock-in-trade, and if it should prove possible to teach these by some planned or mechanical device, what, within their powers, would be left for them to do?

Few educators would fall into the fallacy of thinking that, barring some breakthrough on the front being explored in American Samoa, the new technology, in the forms in which it has been devised in developed countries, will make teaching easier, especially at the primary stages. It should make teaching more effective, but only at the cost of more effort and greater understanding on the part of the teacher. When a technique is devised to operate at stage IV, it is not just a new tool that is being put into the teachers' hands but a new and more complex purpose they are being asked to accept. Given a docile class or a strong disciplinarian, there is no form of teaching that makes less intellectual demand on the teacher than endless drills in the simple skills and in the memorizing of disconnected facts. If educational technology is to be used to lead teachers away from this to something more effective and meaningful, they will have the right to ask for specific

---

[8] E. J. Green's comment on programmed instruction is typical of many statements on the new teaching techniques: "It is not the objective of any program to replace the teacher . . . The program does not make the work of the teacher easier, for, if the program is used effectively, it will provide the teacher with a classroom full of children who are as familiar with the basic didactic material of his subject as he is . . . It is the teacher's task to teach enthusiasm by example." Edward J. Green, *The Learning Process and Programmed Instruction* (New York: Holt, Rinehart and Winston, 1962), p. 136.

guidance on how the new techniques are to replace, or be fused with, their old familiar routines. This involves not only the fitting of the techniques into the daily schedule, and defining the respective functions of the classroom teacher and the television teacher or the program, but also the subtle task, in the years of transition, of what I have called the orchestrating of the old with the new in the classroom. We are not yet in a position to give this guidance from our own experience, and it is not the kind of thing that can be spun from theory. What do we know, for instance, of the problems created for teacher and pupil when the same man in the same classroom tries to teach elementary science at the stage IV level by the problem-solving techniques of ESI, while, without the benefit of external aid, he continues to teach history and geography at stage II by making children copy down a few scrappy notes from the blackboard and learn them by heart? To this and a score of related questions we have no replies, and it is important that, in addition to pilot projects on the introduction of isolated techniques into the schools of emergent countries, we should concern ourselves just as seriously with research into their effects on the role of the teacher and on the whole pattern and tone of the classroom day.

The material and financial difficulties of introducing the new technology into the schools of developing countries are beyond the scope of this book, but it would be unrealistic to consider the professional problems involved in innovations without a passing reference to their cost. It is to keep down the cost of primary education as well as to speed up the reform of the schools that economists and others have suggested the use of a new technology, and yet, strangely enough, very little work has been done on the cost of the proposed innovations in the schools.

The calculation will be complex. It must take into account not only the direct costs of preparing courses, installing and maintaining equipment, and training teachers to use them, but also such secondary costs as providing electricity and remodelling many tropical schools to protect valuable equipment from thieves, vandals, and the weather. This may shift school building costs into a completely new bracket, because it may become impossible for villagers to go on building the schools from local materials. The only economies to set off against these costs will be any increase in the pupil-teacher ratio (which, in primary schools, is often already so high as to make this unlikely), and the increased "productivity" of the schools. This is a variable of which it is notoriously difficult to get an agreed measure, but it should be possible to reach a rough approximation by the use of standardized tests and by a study of the effects, over a period, on pupil-wastage and on the rate of flow through the schools. The calculation will only be complete when an estimate has been made of the costs of achieving the same level of productivity by the alternative method of improving the general education and training of teachers. The International Institute for Educational Planning has begun an inquiry into the costs of introducing the new technology.[9] If the inquiry is deep enough to enable comparison to be made between alternative methods of arriving at the same goal, it is too much to expect quick results from it. In the meantime, our grounds for assuming that the use of the new technology will keep down the cost of primary education are, to say the least, shaky.

The introduction of complex new teaching techniques depends in no small measure on the stability of the teaching force, and this in turn is intimately related to the cost of education.

---

[9] "Summary of the Institute's Proposed Research Programme for 1965–66," I.I.E.P., Paris, September 1964 (mimeographed), p. 6. Since this summary appeared the project has been greatly expanded under the general direction of Wilbur Schramm, of Stanford University, to cover other aspects besides costs. An attempt is being made to describe and evaluate a number of field experiments in the use of the new educational technology in developing countries. The survey may provide answers to some of the questions raised in this and preceding chapters.

In some primary school systems, the wastage of teachers is hardly less serious than the wastage of pupils.[10] Primary teaching in these countries tends to be regarded as the first step on the social and economic ladder, and a low salary is accepted in exchange for the chance of an education beyond the primary level that will open the way to a more lucrative career. This creates problems for the educational administrator. If he gives entrants to the primary service more general education without raising their salaries, he will finish by making them more eligible for other white collar occupations. Even if he concentrates on providing specialized training in pedagogy and the new techniques in order to raise the standard of teaching, he is in danger of having his money and his efforts wasted when they leave the service at the first opportunity. Nor can the factor of motivation be entirely disregarded, even in a profession that is reputed to have more than its share of idealists; if primary teachers are to remain "low-paid, poorly educated, and unqualified," it is perhaps too much to expect all of them to be deeply interested in improving standards in an occupation that many regard only as a temporary stop-gap. So it is that any attempt to improve the quality of teaching in emergent countries must be accompanied by a study of the extent and causes of wastage among teachers, and of the morale of those who remain in the service. Various methods have been suggested for reducing this wastage, and each of these should, perhaps, be made the subject of a field experiment, but, short of evidence to the contrary, it is hard to escape the conclusion that the best way to protect the original investment in the training of primary teachers is to pay them salaries high enough to compete with other occupations. Since salaries constitute the bulk of educational expenditure, nothing could be more calculated to raise the cost of primary schooling.

[10] See, for instance, *Survey of the Status of the Teaching Profession in Africa* (Washington, D.C.: World Confederation of Organizations of the Teaching Profession, 1964), particularly pp. 1–13.

CHAPTER VII

CONCLUSIONS

It would be pleasant in this final chapter to be able to draw practical conclusions from a series of propositions decisively proved in the earlier chapters. This rarely happens in education. The most that can be claimed here is that a prima facie case has been presented for a number of propositions, which are definite enough to permit of conclusions being drawn from them. The underlying theme—the need for a new theory of educational development to enable educators and economists to work together more effectively in planning—does not fall into this category, but there are three other interlocking themes that do. The first is a plea for increased attention to quality in educational planning; the second is concerned with the resistances within a school system to the changes necessary to improve the quality of instruction; the third is the hypothesis of stages through which a system must move in order to achieve a more meaningful education and of the conditions it must meet to reach each stage. (Subsidiary to the last theme is a brief study of modern techniques that might be used to speed up progress through the stages.) The purpose of this chapter is to answer the question, *"If* the major propositions expounded under each of these themes are correct, what consequences follow for planning in emergent countries?" In spite of their hypothetical flavor, I should obviously not draw these conclusions unless I believed them to be substantially correct.

Consequences of two kinds follow from the propositions put forward in the earlier chapters: those concerned with the theory and practice of educational planning generally, and those that affect the strategy and tactics of planning in any single developing country. I shall deal with them in this order.

GENERAL CONCLUSIONS

The most obvious general conclusion to be drawn from this study is that, in spite of a century or more of practical experience, we are still grievously ignorant of how a school system actually develops and need to know a great deal more about it before we can, with complete assurance, advise emergent countries on their broader educational problems. Recent writers have pointed out that, in education, the amount of money spent on research is trivial compared with the vast sums expended on it by industries of relatively minor importance. But it is just too easy to demand more money for research as the panacea. It is already a commonplace of the profession that relatively little use is made in the classroom of the results of educational research even in developed countries.[1] In the emergent countries, we are still far from having digested intellectually the mass of practical experience teachers and administrators have already acquired, and we have not done enough systematic thinking on the subject to be able to identify with any precision the problems on which research is most needed.

One of the reasons why more practical use has not been made of educational research is undoubtedly the complexity of the problems and the relative crudity of the instruments at our disposal; but, if what has been said about stages of development and resistances to change has any validity, the failure

[1] For an analysis of some of the reasons why research has not had a greater effect on teaching practice see: Robert N. W. Travers, "A Study of the Relationship of Psychological Research to Educational Practice," in Robert Glaser, ed., *Training Research and Education* (Pittsburgh: University of Pittsburgh Press, 1962), pp. 525–558.

of research to influence practice may be due in part to the fact that research workers have, with a few notable exceptions, neglected the problem of how educational practices spread. This is just the problem that is of greatest concern to the administrator and the educational reformer, whether they be operating within a single large school system or advising an emergent country on the adoption of new educational techniques.

To the enthusiastic teacher, and to the theorist who advises him, the diffusion of educational ideas and practices is an untidy and unrewarding field of research, where one has to wait too long for results that often can only be labelled as inconclusive. If you have worked out a new teaching technique, there is excitement in trying it out in pilot projects where you have the double advantage of selected teachers and of the Hawthorne effect.[2] The systematic evaluation of results is rather more tedious, and the later dissemination and institutionalizing of the technique can be positively dreary to one who sees nothing creative in it. As H. M. Brickell has said, these are "three distinctly different, irreconcilable processes. The circumstances which are right for one are essentially wrong for the others. . . . People preferring different phases often have an abrasive effect on each other when brought into close contact."[3] It frequently happens that the research worker loses interest at the point where, for the administrator, the experiment begins to be significant. Its success in a pilot

---

[2] This term is sometimes loosely used to mean little more than the effect of novelty, but it has much more significance than this. It is the effect on a group of workers of their becoming the center of attention in an experimental situation. In the case of innovations in teaching methods, the effect is often intensified by personal contact with the enthusiast who invented or introduced the new procedure. These effects naturally weaken and dissipate as the innovation spreads throughout a large school system.

[3] Henry M. Brickell, "State Organization for Educational Change", in Matthew B. Miles, ed., *Innovation in Education* (New York: Bureau of Publications, Teachers College, Columbia University, 1964), pp. 497–498.

project is no guarantee that a teaching technique can be pressed on all teachers in a system, and, even if it can, it will probably need modification for the average and below-average practitioners. This transition from the outstanding to the mediocre is one that the administrator usually has to handle alone, and it is not altogether surprising that promising innovations spread so slowly or simply disappear in a mist of good intentions.

It would be ungracious to write of this diffusion of educational practices without referring to the pioneer work done in this field by Paul Mort and his colleagues, but their researches were carried out almost entirely in the United States[4] and may or may not be relevant to our present purpose. In spite of this body of work, M. B. Miles introduces a 700-page book on innovation with, "Basically the problem is that we do not *understand*—do not know with any clarity or precision the answers to questions about almost every imaginable aspect of innovation in education."[5] Whether or not this be true of developed countries, the field for research into the dissemination of educational practices in emergent countries certainly stands wide open. There are few areas in which research is more necessary, and possibly none where it is more likely to find immediate practical application.

If the thinking up to now has been correct, it is unlikely that research findings on the diffusion of educational practices at stage IV will carry over unchanged to stage II; and methods used to stimulate the process in developed countries may fail in emergent ones. The hypothesis of stages would lead one to

[4] Synopses of this monumental body of work will be found in an article by Paul R. Mort himself, published posthumously as chapter 13 of Miles' *Innovation in Education,* and in Donald H. Ross, *Administration for Adaptability* (New York: Metropolitan Study Council, 1958). Some of Mort's best-known conclusions about the leisurely rate of diffusion of educational practices have been challenged as a result of the much more rapid spread of some modern practices. See Miles, *Innovation in Education,* pp. 3–7.

[5] Miles, *Innovation in Education,* p. 40.

expect that the lower the school system is on the scale the less reliance will the reformer be able to put on the expounding of theories and general principles as the means of getting new teaching practices more widely adopted. It is easy to exaggerate their value even in the most developed systems. Consistent teaching at the stage IV level demands a change of attitude and purpose as well as new techniques, and so cannot be achieved without some understanding of the principles from which it springs, but one of the most disappointing features of education over the past half-century has been the relative failure of theories by their own logic and weight to bring about general changes in classroom practice, however much they might affect the teaching of a few eager and intelligent disciples.[6] Certainly, the most immediately accepted reforms have been those which, like the PSSC physics program,[7] have built their theory into quite detailed guides for practice.

In emergent countries the ineffectiveness of bare theory as an instrument of educational reform is even more marked. It is too much to expect most teachers with a primary or partially completed secondary education to tussle with the turgid language of an educational theory written for another country and to draw from it their own rules for classroom practice. Nor are they any more likely, on the basis of a set of techniques they

[6] "It is possible that the results of research or innovation are likely to be translated into improved practice only when they have become embodied in concrete devices, materials, and other usable products . . . It seems likely that research on instruction will be applied much less frequently when its sole product is principles, conclusions, or scientific laws." A. A. Lumsdaine, in N. L. Gage, ed., *Handbook of Research on Teaching* (Chicago: Rand McNally, 1963), p. 670.

[7] This is a physics program for secondary schools, prepared by the Physical Science Study Committee and now handled by ESI. In 1957–58 there were 8 teachers and 300 students using the course; during 1964–65 there were 5000 teachers and approximately 200,000 students, about 50 percent of the high school students in the United States enrolled in physics. It is also being introduced in many other countries.

have learned, to construct their own theory and apply it to a wider range of situations. Such experience as we have at this level would seem to indicate that the effects of any course of training in a technique can be quite remarkably specific, with very little carryover to related types of work. The use of the so-called "tram-line" courses in which, as the name suggests, "the teachers are carefully prepared to perform in every detail special pre-selected tasks,"[8] has proved extremely effective in raising the standard of stage II teaching in many places, but it does not, of itself, necessarily improve the teacher's practice outside the specific courses for which he has been trained.

Under wise guidance, the additional confidence that teachers get from operating with a "tram-line" course can later be called upon to enable them to undertake teaching that is rather more adventurous, especially in the lower classes of the school where they have no trouble with the subject matter. I understand from correspondents that the Special Centre at Nairobi, which began by producing detailed instructions for quite old-fashioned courses, went on to revolutionize teaching in the lower primary classes of some Kenyan schools.[9] Without wise guidance, the opposite can occur, and the narrow, mechanical methods of a "tram-line" course, just because they are so successful with a limited objective, can clamp down on the schools and become a new orthodoxy, whose resistance to change can be singularly intense. This is, of course, a phenomenon not

[8] This term (which should presumably be "trolley track" in the United States) is explained very briefly in John J. Figueroa, "Teacher Training for Mass Education in Africa," *The Year Book of Education 1963* (London: Evans Brothers, 1963), pp. 564–565.

[9] Since this was written an evaluation of these reforms—now known as the "New Primary Approach"—has been made by Marnixius Hutasoit and Clifford H. Prator, "A Study of the 'New Primary Approach' in the Schools of Kenya." This survey was carried out in February–March 1965 at the request of the Ministry of Education, and is in mimeographed form. It tends to confirm the reports of my correspondents, but warns about the difficulties of extending the scheme too rapidly with inadequately prepared teachers. See also "Kenya Education Commission Report", part I, Simeon H. Ominde, Chairman (Nairobi, 1964).

confined to education or to developing countries; it is a danger attendant on "systems" in most areas of human endeavor. From their very nature some of the more systematic of the newer teaching techniques seem particularly exposed to this danger. Research on the best methods of applying them in school systems at stage II and the lower end of stage III should be accompanied by correlative research on how to help a system break away from the form of the technique proper to any stage as soon as the teachers are ready for the increased freedom of the next higher stage.

Those who advocate the spending of much greater sums on educational research are, of course, quite right, and, with the example of the physical sciences before us, there is probably no need to make the obvious point that a reasonable proportion of the money must be spent on researches that have no immediate application to classroom practice anywhere. My only plea here is for more systematic and scholarly attention to the novel and peculiar problems of education in emergent countries and particularly to the factors affecting the diffusion of improved methods of teaching. Without it, those of us who are concerned with technical assistance to education in these countries must continue to wear our current title of "educational expert" with mild embarrassment. Some experts have behind them the accumulated practical experience of a lifetime, but even this is rarely broad enough for the jobs with which they are faced; they need as well the systematized thinking and wisdom of a profession.

CONCLUSIONS AT COUNTRY LEVEL

It remains finally to draw from the hypothesis of stages and the pattern of resistances to change in a school system the consequences for the strategy and tactics of educational planning in any emergent country. Only those aspects of planning will be touched upon which would be affected by the acceptance or rejection of the point of view on these subjects expressed in previous chapters. This means that only peripheral attention will be given to manpower planning in the normally accepted sense, but the approach does have the virtue of concentrating our attention on those parts of planning in which the educator must play the leading role, or in which, at least, his contribution must carry weight. If it is permitted to mix medical terms with military, the subject will be treated under three headings: Diagnosis, Strategy, Tactics.

Diagnosis. If a country's plan for education is to be part of its economic and social planning, the educational administrator's first task is to assess the potentiality for growth of his school system. If there is any truth in the theories that have been advanced, this educational diagnosis cannot wait until the economic plan is complete. It is not the educator's sole function to suggest ways and means of carrying out the educational sector of a readymade plan, for information that only he can find may affect, if not the ends of the over-all plan, at least its timing. If the problem were purely quantitative, it might be possible for a layman to make an estimate of the time it will take to erect x buildings, train y teachers, and produce an output of z graduates at any level of the school system. But, as is seen at every turn, quantity and quality are inextricably linked in education, and the speed at which the quality of the work can be improved depends in large measure on the attitudes and the level of preparation of the teachers in the schools. Unless skilled workers are to be imported on a grand scale to make up deficiencies, the demand of the national plan for educated manpower must be related to the maximum rate of growth, in both quality and quantity, of the education system. So the educator's diagnosis is essential both in setting up the over-all plan and in devising the tactics for carrying out his part of it.

For present purposes it will be assumed that the records of the Ministry of Education will contain all the raw data necessary to give the quantitative picture of the school system. This, it must be said, is by no means always the case, and the information the official records do contain is not necessarily very accurate. Even if what one might call the static picture is tolerably correct, it is highly improbable that the records will give any reliable indication of the rate of flow of pupils through the schools, and this is a major factor in assessing the efficiency of primary schools in many emergent countries. These difficulties, however, exist whether or not one accepts the thesis of stages of development of a school system, and they can be ignored here except insofar as they are intensified by the results of the qualitative assessment.

In making his qualitative diagnosis the educator would be greatly helped if he could set the school system within some such framework as is provided by the hypothesis of stages. To make the argument more concrete, I shall assume that the scale of stages set out in the chart on page 72 is sufficiently validated to be used for this purpose. The first step is to assess the position of the school system on this scale, fixing both the stage reached by the average teachers and the spread along the scale. Even with the rough criteria provided in Chapter III and in the chart, this is not impossible; if the criteria could be refined and even expressed numerically, the fixing of the points on the scale would be facilitated, and it would, moreover, be possible to check the judgments of independent observers against one another. The educational planner next makes an inventory of the level of general education and of the amount of training of the teachers in the service.

At this point an extremely interesting comparison can be made between different school systems. I think, for instance, of two systems I have seen, in both of which the average level of teaching, as nearly as I could judge, was at the top of stage II. Yet the teachers in Country A had no more than a grade VI or VII education and either one or two years of teacher training, while the average teacher in Country B had what passed for a secondary education. One could not but feel that the teachers in Country B were teaching below their capacity, and that a less wooden administration and some efficient training in techniques could produce teaching at least half a stage higher. In country A, the educational authorities were giving lively leadership, and the majority of the teachers were probably doing about as well as they could with their inadequate level of general education. Such personal judgments are possibly unreliable without more rigorous enquiry, but they serve to illustrate the contention that any attempt to increase the productivity of a school system without a diagnosis of the quality of the instruction, and of the factors determining it, can result in a great deal of wasted effort.

We do not as yet know enough about the limits put on the average teacher's practice by his own level of general education to be able to predict with confidence the ceiling of performance for any given body of teachers—and there are always, happily, unusual individuals who will confound any prediction. But if experiments and controlled observation of the types sketched in the preceding chapter were undertaken systematically, it should be possible to discover the stage of practice normally reached by the average teacher with a given level of general education,[10] and, more hopefully, the stages the same kind of people can achieve with the help of both

[10] There is, of course, no suggestion that increases in the general level of education of teachers will necessarily continue indefinitely to result in improved classroom practice. There may well be a ceiling beyond which further increments of general education have no effect at all. If there is anything in the theory of the "gap" between the teacher's knowledge and that of his pupils, the ceiling may vary with the grade level at which the teaching is being done. This borders on quite a different question: if the teacher's level of general education is one of the major factors determining his ability to improve his teaching practice, why is it that secondary school teachers have the reputation of being more conservative than their primary school colleagues? The theory of the "gap" may be a partial explanation, but the full story is much more complex than that, and calls for a separate study of professional conservatism at the secondary level.

the older and the newer techniques of teaching. (For reasons given earlier, the brilliant individual and the pilot project with selected teachers would have to be ignored for this purpose.) It would be foolish to pretend that all this will be easy. In any system, the results will be confused by other factors: the material conditions of the schools, the attitudes of parents and public, and the skill and liveliness of administrators and professional leaders. These should not interfere, however, with the determination of the highest level of practice that is, in fact, under favorable conditions achieved by a large group of teachers with a certain level of general education. More difficult will be the establishment of valid measures and criteria of achievement and improvement in a school system. Attempts to evaluate the results of experiments with new teaching methods in developed countries have usually been depressingly inconclusive, partly because of the crudeness of the measuring instruments and partly as a result of failure to agree on just what constitutes progress. In emergent countries, where the failings of the school system are more evident, the measurement of improvement may be easier; educators are more likely to agree on the changes to be made in classroom practice, and the progress achieved as a result of using new methods may be obvious enough to be measured by coarsely calibrated instruments or judged by skilled and impartial observers.

However difficult the task, it must be attempted if the qualitative component of educational planning is ever to carry the weight it should. An educator who was able to assess the stage of practice reached by a body of teachers with a given amount of education and training, and then to compare that with the best standards known to have been achieved by a similar, unselected body of teachers, would be in a fair position to estimate his school system's capacity for improvement, and, in addition perhaps, to form an opinion on how the reforms might be brought about and how long they should take.

Whether the decision would be to begin the reforms by increasing the general education of the teachers or by concentrating on specific professional training would depend not only on his diagnosis but also on a series of factors beyond his control, such as the amount of money available, and the urgency of the country's need for graduates at each level. At this point where educational strategy is to be decided, political, economic, and social goals may be of paramount importance to those in charge of the over-all national plan, and the educator must have a clear idea of his functions in the planning process.

Strategy. The educator must realize that rarely, if ever, will he be the person to make the final decision on broad educational strategy, and the government, which usually retains that privilege for itself, will not necessarily even regard him as the final adviser to whom it turns before determining its policy. When deciding what proportion of the national budget to devote to education, it is more likely to seek counsel from the economist (whether he be Treasury official or professional adviser) because he is the technical expert with the widest range of interest in the field of finance. For manpower problems, it may rely on a group of specialists of whom the educator is unlikely to be the most influential. On policies such as the elimination of illiteracy, where political pledges or the country's international image are concerned, the government's own political sense and judgment may, rightly or wrongly, outweigh the advice of any expert. At the stage of diagnosis, the educator, whatever aid he gets from statisticians, may rightly claim to be the authority, and at the point where tactics are being worked out to put a policy into operation he should be the leading professional figure, although so dependent is he on finance and on government approvals that he will be free to make his own unfettered judgments only within a narrow professional sphere. At the intermediate stage, where educational strategy is in question, the educator must reconcile himself to a less authoritative role.

This is far from agreeing that the educator can be eliminated from the planning of strategy or that he can be nudged into an observer's seat in the background. His contribution to any discussion may never be the final one, but it can be vital to the decision. Not only is his diagnosis of the potential of the school system essential, but he may have other contributions to make to national planning that will come as a surprise to those whose stereotype of the educator vaguely resembles Mr. Chips. Teachers and administrators, for example, who have spent their lives in technical education and in close contact with industry may have much to offer to the manpower specialist confronted with the perennial problem of what kind and level of education is the minimum necessary for any given occupation. Some educators are toughened administrators who will adapt themselves with little effort to the work of a planning committee composed mostly of politicians, economists, and men-of-affairs. Others have led more secluded lives and may feel lost in such company and overawed by the problems they meet or by the language in which they are couched, but their contribution to the strategy of education is so important that, if economically and politically sophisticated educators cannot be found in sufficient number to take part in over-all planning, we must train some.

The best way to give reality to the argument and bring it back to the central theme of the significance of the hypothesis of stages of development is to list some of the questions that must be asked when educational strategy is being determined within the framework of a national plan. Three major questions will suffice to illustrate the point:

A. *What proportion of the national budget shall be allocated to education?* Logically, the answer to this question should depend, in large measure though not exclusively, on the answer to question B, but, in view of the amount of interest it arouses, it can take first place.

B. *What demand shall the national plan make on the educational system?* This covers primarily the demands for educated and trained manpower from each level of the school system, but it will also include any more diffuse demands the plan may make for such things as a greater interest within the community in science, industry, or agriculture, a more practical understanding of the meaning and mechanisms of democracy, or a keener sense of national unity.

C. *In very broad terms, how shall these demands be met?* To help distinguish between "strategic" and "tactical" questions of this type, it may be useful to suggest two or three questions that could poperly be asked when strategy is being decided. Would a mass literacy campaign among adults help to meet the manpower needs? Of the limited monies available, what proportion should be spent on the extension of primary schooling, and what on secondary and higher education? If extra funds are available for primary education, should the emphasis be on a rapid increase in the number of pupils or on the improvement in the quality of the instruction?

These are all questions in which the educator is intensely interested, but so are other people, and their arguments may outrank his. There would seem to be five major functions the educator might be expected to have in a team planning educational strategy at this level. The first and last of the functions set out below would not be greatly affected whether the educator accepted or rejected the thesis of stages of development of a school system, but they are affected by other views expressed earlier in this book. The functions of the educator at this stage of planning are:

(1) He must represent—in truth fight for—the interests of education, and strive to ensure that it gets its rightful place in the national plan and its fair share of the budget. Planning

is not, and probably never will be, a purely rational process, and, when all the available facts have been fed into the computer and all the conclusions drawn, much will still depend upon the balance struck between competing interests, and upon the tenacity and skill of the men who defend each of them. There will be a host of rival claims—nearly all of them praiseworthy—for the limited amount of money that will be available over the planning period. Schools, hospitals, roads, dams, factories, farms, social services, defense—all will have their protagonists, each with his passionate sense of priorities. The politician or economist, or whoever is chosen as having the least obvious set of sectional interests, will finish by weighing not facts in a vacuum but facts embedded in competing claims. I see no cause to lament this procedure, which prevails in most countries, and which often produces a plan more acceptable to the country as a whole than the pure product of human intellect, but I do see in it a reason why the educator, representing as he does some of the vital interests of a whole generation, should stay as close as possible to the place where policy decisions are made. The exact point at which he will make his influence felt will depend upon his status. If he is himself a politician, he may exercise his persuasion at Cabinet level, and if a career administrator he will keep the claims of education firmly before his minister or before any planning commission.

The foreign adviser on education would do well to avoid direct pressure at either of these points, but he will probably have to represent, in a more than passive sense, the interests of education among his colleagues in an advisory mission, and he will certainly help to prepare material that his opposite number in the national administration will use to forward the cause of education. In an administration where policy is determined not only by facts but by the method of presenting them and by the resolution of diverging lines of forces, the educator cannot afford to leave to anyone else the task of defending the claims of education before the final planning authority. So long as he relies on reasoned argument and not on political maneuvering even the scholarly planner loses none of his dignity or intellectual integrity by pressing, firmly and in the right place, the case for education. In a very real sense, this is a part of planning. It should be needless to add that, once the plan is officially promulgated, the educator must adhere to it loyally, whether or not his point of view prevails.

(2) A second function of the educator is to keep the manpower expert informed on the practicability of the demands being made on the educational system for graduates at each level. This is one of the main reasons for the quantitative and qualitative diagnosis of the system; the diagnosis will obviously depend in some degree on the truth of the hypothesis of stages. It may well be that the economic planner will be justified in fixing an industrial manpower target rather higher than the maximum output forecast for the schools would seem to indicate, and that for two reasons. In the first place, in many industries partly educated workers can be substituted for fully educated workers more readily than is often imagined. Secondly, no one can be dogmatic over a period of years in forecasting the exact output of the schools, and, if real pressure is put on them, the figure may show a moderate rise. Nevertheless, if, as sometimes happens, the manpower demands of the economic plan are out of all relation to the capacity of the schools as shown by the educator's diagnosis, the results are no less serious than if the plan were based on a grievous error in the supply of power or raw materials.

(3) When the planning authority comes to make strategic decisions of the type listed under question C above, the obvious duty of the educator is to point out, as well as he is able, the probable consequences of each of the alternatives before the authority. Let us take the last of the questions on this list

as an example. The government can decide to spend any additional money it has for the primary schools on a swift increase in the numbers or on an intensive effort to improve the quality of the product. While being sensitive to the complex of political, economic, and humanitarian factors that determine the government's final choice of routes, the educator must regard it as his prime responsibility to forecast what will lie at the end of each.

Let us suppose that his preliminary diagnosis has shown that the majority of the teachers are operating toward the upper end of stage II, but that some have broken into stage III and an adventurous handful of teachers in the lower grades of some schools are experimenting with more meaningful teaching near stage IV. He knows that, if the teaching force must be rapidly expanded, the product of the secondary schools will not be sufficient to provide him with teacher-trainees with a reasonably good general education. Nor will he be able to dam up the flow of trained recruits for a year or two while he extends the two-year teacher-training course to help make good this educational deficiency. So he must rely on an inflow of teachers with little more than a primary education and, with luck, two years of "professional" training. If there is anything in the hypothesis of stages of development, he realizes that this will limit the teaching of the great bulk of teachers to stage II, unless, by some minor miracle of stimulation and special training or techniques, he can produce results with the new teachers that he has failed to produce with the majority of the existing ones.

The government or the planning authority may not be particularly interested in his professional reasoning so far; what they are concerned with are the numbers and kinds of people the schools can produce within the planning period. He may be wise to begin by explaining that, with the new influx of ill-educated teachers, there is probably nothing he can do to improve the already excessive rate of pupil-wastage and to speed up the flow of pupils through the system. So some of the new money they intend to pour into the schools will almost certainly be wasted if rapid expansion is adopted as the policy.

He may find it more difficult to explain that the average product of a school at stage II tends to be a different *kind* of person from the pupil who has graduated from a school at stage IV or the upper level of stage III. Long years of poor teaching, boredom, rote memorizing, dependence on authority, and vague connections between symbols and their meanings can scarcely be regarded as the ideal preparation for the majority of citizens of a country that is struggling belatedly into the twentieth century, with all the tensions and problems resulting from rapid industrial growth, a revolution in agriculture, the establishment of a democratic form of government, and the inevitable conflict between old and new sets of values. Mass education at a stage II level may be adequate for the needs of a certain kind of static society, and it may be all that some countries faced with major changes can hope, for the moment, to achieve, in which case the burden—and the privileges—of change will tend to fall to an educated elite.

If the government should choose the other, and harder, alternative of spending most of the extra funds available for primary education on improving the quality of instruction, the picture drawn by the educator will be very different. The "tooling-up" period will be long and expensive. New entrants to teaching will need to be given a full secondary education, and that will not only delay their entrance to a school of education but will also deprive industry and the government services of secondary school graduates they need immediately. New problems of buildings, equipment, salaries, and teaching techniques come under the heading of tactics rather than strategy, but the educator will need to foresee them clearly even at this stage if he is to tell the government what price it must pay in money and time to buy the kind of education really fitted to a modern society.

Here this particular function of the educator stops. He will have his own opinions on which alternative should be chosen, and, because of his professional interest in quality, he will probably be biased toward the second. There is no reason why he should not, in the appropriate places, argue the case for the route of his choice, but he must accept the fact that the final decision will not be purely, or even predominantly, an educational one.

(4) The educator's fourth function at the level of strategy is to offer an estimate of how long each change contemplated by the planning authority will take, and how much it will cost. This is a special case of the third function, and it is treated separately here only because of the importance these two factors assume in any plan. For the estimate of cost the educator may call in outside specialists, but it is an extension of a relatively routine function that an administrator carries out regularly, and any reasonably efficient ministry of education should be equipped to handle it. The time taken to plan, build, and equip schools is also based on well-known practice, though both time and cost may be modified by the adoption of novel designs and materials. It is when he comes to estimate the time for the training of teachers that the educator's professional skill and judgment become completely essential and that he feels the need of some such schema as the four stages of development.

Under any conditions, what I have called the "tooling-up" period is likely to be lengthy. If the authorities are willing to accept the miserable standards of the lower levels of stage II, they may get quick results of a kind by putting primary school graduates back into the schools as teachers without any training, and the length of the tooling-up period will depend mostly on the speed at which buildings can be put up and equipped. If teaching at the upper levels of stage II is aimed at, it may perhaps be achieved by giving these same recruits a couple of years of teacher training, and, if new techniques can be found, the standard reached may be somewhat higher than stage II. Already the time-lag for extending the school system will have stretched appreciably, for, in many emergent countries, before great numbers of teachers can be trained it is necessary to train the people who will train them, and the devising and trying out of new techniques can be very time-consuming. The moment one demands teaching at stage IV or at the upper levels of stage III, the time-lag may double or treble, for now it is a matter of giving the recruits a full secondary education, and of training more teachers and erecting schools at this level also. For reasons of space, I may have given a spurious air of accuracy to the calculations the educator can do in estimating the time it will take for the school system to reach each of the stages, but any experienced administrator is accustomed to making judgments not very different from this, and already has an understanding of the inexorable chain of events—plans, financial approvals, buildings, recruitment, training—that precedes every expansion and most reforms. Once he knows what the planning authorities are thinking of asking of the schools, he is in a better position than anyone else to say how long it will take to deliver the product.

(5) The last major function of the educator when strategy is under review is one which, with more cunning than courage, I have so far avoided. In Chapter I, I chose a definition of "quality" in education that was restricted enough to invite no discussion on the ultimate goals of education. This concept served tolerably well for the examination of the stages of development of a school system, but it is not enough to meet the purposes of the educator sitting in conference with politicians, economists, industrialists, and manpower experts to recom-

mend a broad strategy for education within a national plan. As parent and citizen every man around the table will have his own ideas on schooling, and there is no reason to believe that the achievement of the good life as the aim of education is the ideal of the educator alone, or that he is the sole defender of the moral and aesthetic values of society. The only difference between the educator and the rest is that he is the only man there whose *professional* duty it is to think first of all of the interests of the child.

To represent these interests steadily in a sophisticated group wrestling with the complex problems of national planning is by no means an easy task. Every educator has seen the glaze come over the eyes of an audience after a few minutes of exposure to the higher aims of education, and the term "frills" stands as a linguistic monument to what some of our fellow-citizens think of our efforts to introduce children to the arts. Knowing this, the educator is open to two dangers when he descends from the rostrum and sits as an equal with members of other professions discussing a plan for education. He may lean over backwards to avoid the charge of woolly idealism (I have done so in this book), and concentrate his attention on something he thinks of as "education for economic development," or he may, with schoolmasterish air, behave as if he were dealing with Philistines instead of with men no less cultured than himself whose minds are, for the moment, fixed on other goals. Somewhere between these two attitudes lies his professional obligation to remind himself and others from time to time that the child, like the man, does not live by bread alone. This duty is the more imperative since the educator may find himself obliged to represent the views of other professionals—sociologists, anthropologists, artists—who, unlike him, have no official place in the planning establishment.

It might appear that this is an academic discussion with little relevance to planning education in an emergent country

where the material needs are so overwhelming as truly to reduce to "frills" any parts of education that do not cater directly
to meeting them. Nothing could be farther from the truth. If
there is anything I have learned from dealing with educational
leaders in emergent countries over the past twenty years, it is
that you neglect at your peril the culture of a country and the
contribution it can make to education. Little of this may show
in the work of the schools, and the parents in the villages may
clamor for the bread-and-butter schooling that will help their
children to get a job in a government office, but those who
speak for their countries are often fiercely resistant to any
suggestion that, because of their poverty, their plans for education should be strictly utilitarian. In part, this may spring
from a philosophy of life that is less material than ours (the
claim is theirs, not mine), but it is an attitude that has been
strengthened by the flow of material and technical aid from
developed to emergent countries since the war. It is natural
that a country with an ancient culture, which has, for ten or
fifteen years, been the constant recipient of aid and advice
from wealthier lands, should become sensitive about this role
and should lay increasing stress on what it feels to be its
unique contribution to world culture and to the education of
its own children. Countries, like many in Africa, whose history and culture have been unwritten or obscured are search-
ing back for the roots of their civilization to give the dimension of time to their national consciousness and to have
something of their own to pass on to a new generation.[11] So
it may happen that, when the educator in the meeting of
planners presses the claims of aspects of education not directly
related to economic development, he will not only be repre-

[11] The leaders of African nations south of the Sahara fought passionately
at the General Conference of UNESCO in 1960 for the preservation of the
Nubian monuments threatened by the Aswan Dam, and refused to be de-
flected from their purpose by suggestions that money might be better spent
on schools. The Nubian monuments were not, in any rigorous sense, a part
of their own history, but they were a part of *their* continent.

senting the interests of the children but will also be taking a line that is politically hard-headed.

Tactics. There are some who maintain that the implementation of a plan is, in itself, no part of planning. To show my disagreement with this point of view, I have headed this section "tactics" rather than "implementation." The difference between tactics and strategy is one of degree, of distance from the front line, and carries no implication that the business of planning ceases when the broad lines of policy appear in the printed five-year plan. Rarely is the over-all plan for education couched in terms definite enough for its implementation to be no more than the carrying out of fixed instructions; where it is as definite as this, experience in the field frequently shows parts of it to be impracticable, and the educational administrator must go back to the planning authority for fresh guidelines. In doing so he makes his own recommendations for amendments and so comes back again into the main planning stream. Educational planning is a continuous process, and the educator is in it from the beginning to the end. One of the common complaints of developing countries is that foreign advisers leave them as soon as the broad strategy of a plan has been determined, and seldom stay to see it tested and amended by practice.

Since tactics extend to matters of detail, it would be tedious to adopt here the method used in the section on strategy of listing the questions to be answered by the educator. All I am concerned to do is to assess the relevance of the thesis put forward in earlier chapters to the problems the educator meets at this stage. Most of the points have already been covered, and, for the rest, the conclusions to be drawn are so obvious as to need only bare mention. So what follows is little more than a checklist of the principles emerging from this study which are of relevance for the educator carrying out his part of a national plan. Since the chief concern throughout has been with the qualitative rather than the quantitative problems of education, it is natural that the same bias will show at this stage of the argument, but this is in no way intended to minimize the difficulties that sheer numbers can create for the educator. The problems involved in providing new buildings, equipment, and services in an emergent country are often immense, but, from the point of view of theory, they are routine, and call for no comment here.

It is when he comes to find the numbers of teachers called for by the plan that the educator faces problems that are as much qualitative as quantitative. The broad decision on the amount of general education and professional training to be given to the mass of the primary teachers will have been taken at the level of strategy, and the number of buildings and faculty needed to train them will have been calculated. His earlier diagnosis of the system, and such theory of stages as may have been substantiated, will enable the administrator to estimate the stage of teaching practice which should be reached by teachers with the amount of education and training decided upon. From then on his chief tactical problem is to provide the conditions under which the practice of each teacher in the service can most nearly reach the ceiling set by his qualities and qualifications. It is possible that some of the principles suggested by this study might be of value to him here.

A relevant principle to be drawn from the hypothesis of stages is that, for teachers, if not for educational philosophers, the goals of education are emergent, in the sense that they must be within the range of the teachers' capabilities, and will evolve as those capabilities expand. The more clearly the teachers can be made to see the immediate goals, the more likely they are to make them their own, and eventually to approach them and then see other goals beyond them.[12] To

---

[12] There are probably some inspired teachers who, from the upper slopes of stage IV, have already glimpsed stage V, a vision revealed, as yet, to few administrators.

set a goal that is too distant may only be to confuse an inadequately prepared teacher, but, on the other hand, a temporary goal that is too easily achieved tends to become an end in itself, and constant pressure is necessary to keep the system on the move. One of the best ways of doing this is to encourage the ablest and liveliest of the teachers constantly to experiment and break new ground, but here the administrator comes up against the problem, mentioned earlier, of devising a system of control flexible enough to give freedom to some teachers while providing the rest with the degree of authoritative support they need to feel secure in their work. It is most difficult at stage II, where ill-educated teachers are most in need of a supporting framework of fixed curricula, official texts, external examinations, and inspection, which tend, in a large school system at this stage, to become unyielding and universal. The rigidity of the system is intensified if, as usually happens, there is at the end of the primary school an external examination giving access to a limited number of secondary school places, because the natural conservatism of the teachers is then reinforced by the parents' fear that any experiment with new methods may jeopardize their children's chances.

Any attempt to reform the work in the classroom is most likely to succeed if it is part of a nationwide movement for the improvement of social and economic conditions, if it is known to be warmly supported by the ministry of education at all levels as well as by the teachers' own organizations, if steps have been taken to make the parents understand the changes, and if the teacher can be made to feel himself less isolated in his classroom. All this is well-known to an experienced administrator; what is not quite so obvious is that the effect common to all these factors is the added sense of security in a changing situation which they give to the teacher. It is hardly necessary to add—though it is sometimes forgotten—that the reformer's efforts will be largely wasted if the salaries and conditions of service of the primary teachers are not such as to retain good people in the profession.

Having set the stage for the reforms called for under the plan, the educational administrator can now give more attention to teaching methods, curricula, textbooks, equipment, and training courses adapted to the levels of both teachers and children in the school system. These problems have been the theme of a major portion of this study, and the only way to add to what has already been said would be to go into detail quite beyond the scope of such a work. We are still not in a position to advise the administrator in an emergent country whether or not he can hope to find eventually a new and cheap educational technology with which to get more effective teaching from ill-educated teachers, but we can tell him, with some assurance, that he would be unwise to base his planning for the next five or ten years on the assumption that such help will be forthcoming on a grand scale. In the meantime we should bend all our efforts to proving this melancholy prediction wrong.

Writing as an educator, I have tried to outline the function of my profession in the business of educational planning. It is almost inevitable that such a study should show evidence of bias, but the fact that I have made no attempt to sketch the functions of the economists or of any other professional group in the process means only that I have no competence to do so. There are many opinions in this essay that can, as yet, be expressed only tentatively, but of two things I am completely certain: more attention must be given to the quality of education in developing countries, and there must be closer professional cooperation between the educator and the economist in educational planning. If the two professions ignore or disagree with each other in developed countries, it will be a pity but not a tragedy. There will be others to weigh our competing arguments and make the final decisions. In the emergent countries the system of checks and balances may be less effective, and our joint responsibility so much the greater. On occasion we may have to give advice that will be politically unpalatable, and it will be listened to only if economists and educators speak with one voice. We have a great deal of work to do together before we can.

INDEX

INDEX